Wondr

The Faery F

Kay Mullin

Wondrous Land
The Faery Faith of Ireland

ISBN 1 86163 010 7

Cover design by Paul Mason
Cover and internal illustrations by Cormac Figgis

Published by:

Capall Bann Publishing
Freshfields
Chieveley
Berks
RG20 8TF

Dedication

To Marjorie Watson, who believed in me before I believed in myself.

The extracts from the main manuscript collection and the Schools' manuscript collection of the Department of Irish Folklore at University College Dublin are published by kind permission of the Acting Head of Department. The extracts from *Stories and Traditions from Iveragh*, and *Fairy Legends from Donegal* are published by kind permission of the Folklore of Ireland Council, and the extracts from Béaloideas are published by kind permission of the Folklore of Ireland Society.

The extract from *In Search of Biddy Early* by Edmond Lenihan published by Mercier Press, 5 French Church Street, Cork, Ireland are published by the kind permission of the Mercier Press.

The extract from Bunting's Ancient Music of Ireland, edited from the original manuscripts by Donal O'Sullivan with Mícheál Ó Súilleabháin, Cork University Press, Cork, Ireland, are published by kind permission of the Cork University Press.

Acknowledgments

To compile a complete list of contributors would be a long but grateful effort, as so many along the way have contributed so very much, and continue to do so. Thus the following list is only partial.

Thanks to my colleagues Cormac Figgis and Gabriel Rosenstock of Dublin. Cormac's inspired illustrations and Gabriel's miraculous poetic talents grace the pages of the book to the delight of us all - including the Kingdom of faerie. To Minette Quick who has given constant support, to Noelle Coleman who showed me the faithful kindness and competence of an Irish hostess, to Jim Grant who has assisted me in countless ways. To Hal Zina Bennett, Jane Crane, Viva Knight, and Aedin McLoughlin for their essential editorial services and friendship; to my good-humored and bolstering agent Grahame Maclean; a special thanks to Cathal Ó Searcaigh and Seán Ó hEochaidh whose contributions greatly enriched the book. To Irish friends Liam Breslin, the DeChant family, Carol O'Callaghan, Jaya Moran, Michael Morris, Brendon O'Donnell, Juliet Purser, Patricia Swann; to the crew at Baile Chonnail.

To Rosemarie Anderson, George Beck, Daryl and Annioelle Carlson and the late Flower Newhouse of Questhaven Retreat, Susan D'Aoust, Sally and Kenny Eyer, Mark Landau, Ron Rosenstock, and Scott S. Smith who carry the faery-faith well in America. Also Kinsley Jarrett and Jenny O'Dwyer of Australia, William Bloom of London and the Findhorn Community in Scotland, Mitzi Huxley and the National Fairy Appreciation Society of England.

My thanks to Jim Bryne, Christy Nolan, Willie White, Charles, Sue, and Simon of County Carlow; Michael Barrett, James Lee, and Delia O'Toole of County Connemara; Paddy and Nora Bonner, Vincent Campbell, John Henderson, Sergeant Kelly, Joseph Logue, Ellen McGarvey, Mary and Tom McGinley, Pádraic, Mary and Pat Walsh of County Donegal; Patrick Francis of County Dublin; Bob Ferriter, Ted Moriarty of County Kerry; Marita Lyons of County Meath; and Michael Dowling of County Wicklow for teaching me the ways of faerie.

To Billie Ogden and Paul Tuttle and their gentle guides Jeramiah and Raj who continue to show me the way, for the wisdom offered through A Course in Miracles and the Pathwork. To Mother Meera.

To my mother Dorothy for her Irish ways and to my father Samuel for his Celtic insights - knowing he would have so much enjoyed all of this had he stayed a bit longer. To my daughters and family - Shelly and Brent, Lynn and Kevin, Debra and Michael, and my grandchildren in order of appearance - Ryan, Ian, Christine, Sammy, Taylor, Patrick, Kristin - for their enthusiasm.

Contents

I

A Grand Adventure

Will you come with me,
To the wondrous land where harmony is.
Hair is like the crown of the primrose

and the body smooth and white as snow.
A wondrous land is the land I tell of.

Etain (Irish, Ninth century)

If, as a child, I had a faery godmother to grant me a wish, I would have asked for a grand adventure. I was to get that wish, but not for many decades.

It was on my birthday and the first night of the Full August Moon 1991 that I arrived in Ireland. There was magic in the clean, clear air and something almost musical in the silence that lay on the land and in the way the many shades of green basked in the silvery light. I knew I was close to the door of the Otherworld. My grand adventure was about to begin.

If this all sounds a bit like a faery story that's not surprising, because that is what it is, only it is a real faery story, about real faeries. For faeries and elves and gnomes are indeed quite real, even though they are not made of material matter as are we. Let me tell you how the faery tale began.

Once upon a time, I was a well-established clinical psychologist in the Monterey bay area of California and I had for some time been visiting a medium there who channelled advice to me. During the consultation, I asked about my new-born granddaughter, Christine Kay.

"She is from the faery kingdom. A very healing being, who is able to see into many dimensions of reality other than this one," the voice declared. "She will do much good for the world, if she is allowed to be who she is." I was astonished-but about to be more so, for the voice continued: "You are also from the faery kingdom also, and you have some work to do if you will accept the challenge."

With that announcement, time was up. I was left with a lot of unanswered questions. Yes, I could have gone along with my little Christine being psychic - Irish on her mother's side, Scots on her father's side. Generations of our family had talked about the second sight, and it was not unusual for us to have conversations with psychics, mediums, fortune tellers, or whatever. But faeries?

Puzzled, I called up my friend Sally Eyer who had recommended the medium to me. Billie Ogden was transmitting the voice, which she claimed came from sources beyond this dimension. Billie was a stable, intelligent woman well thought of by those who consulted her. She was part of the grid of intuitive or psychic guidance that has always been around, but the display of it was certainly accelerating by the mid-1970s in certain areas of America. Channelled messages varying in quality and content, but with the same underlying message, are now being received all over the globe. The message is this:

The world is waking up and is going to change very much in the times to come. We have lost contact with our Source, but we are regaining it. Our true nature is divine. Spirituality is meant to be a joyful experience. We have let scientific materialism nearly strangle the magic out of life, but it has not succeeded. The rational is the servant rather than the master. The intuitive is the call to mystery.

2

These ideas were familiar to us. Sally and her husband Ken had been lifelong friends of mine, and we readily shared our experiences with this form of communication.

"What kind of a source is coming through Billie? Is that one a sick comedian? Everything was really helpful during most of the conversation, and then at the last minute the voice said that I'm from the faeries. Isn't that embarrassing? So is my granddaughter, according to what was said."

Both of them dissolved into gleeful laughter, defending their friend Billie's integrity. *"But of course you are a faery, what else could you be? That explains you. We've known you since you were little, and you have always been funny, amusing, playing tricks, all those things faeries do. Light, great sense of humour. A hybrid."*

"Well, the humour is missing now, " I replied glumly. "That strange one said I have some work to do."

"It's some kind of challenge. You'll always wonder about it if you let it go. Do it."

Sally was right. My curiosity was aroused. I continued to have conversations with the energy speaking through Billie for about a year. The often rambling dialogues were interspersed with personal agendas, but the message did not vary. Other intuitive counsellors also agreed, and this voice is referred to as Spirit throughout this book. [1]

The hope is that the handful of us who are coming into the awareness of what we have evolved from would make a commitment, and do whatever was needed to make known the reality of the faery kingdom.

The work would be to create a passage - opening the doorway - between mankind and the faery kingdom. For until the awareness is there, neither can complete their potential. When all the kingdoms - seen and unseen - come in awareness and acceptance of each other, then there will be peace on earth.

Each of us who have an affinity with the nature kingdoms potentially has a piece of the doorway, and when we come together and put the pieces in place the doorway will open. It will be a portal of peace, a portal of love. Even though the elemental world is humourous and light-hearted, we have closed the door to their presence. The door needs to be opened from this side.

There would be others involved in the re-claiming of the faery kingdom, Spirit said, so although my assignment might be strange, at least it wouldn't be solitary. In the beginning I was worried, it might seem as if we are out on a twig - let alone a limb. We would be forerunners, pioneers. "Do not forget that this is your assignment," Spirit told me. "This is what you came here to do."

What I was being told to do was simple enough, and if I had done it without resistance, it would have been far easier to accomplish. I was to be one of those who would write the truth about the faery kingdom.

This required to research, first-hand, and the best possible place to do this was Ireland. Mystical Ireland, where all of my grandparents were born, where my parents had spent summers in their retirement years, and where my children had vacationed with them.

"Mother, you would love it there. I was very young when I was there with your folks, but I'll never forget it," my youngest daughter Lynn said to me. "The beauty, the quietness, the gentleness of the people."

Yes, I know that now. But it took a massive inner battle, characterised by doubt and embarrassment to get me there. In retrospect I realise that some kind of inner truth in me was being awakened, but I didn't know it then. Nor would I have listened to myself.

Aspects of the project were congruent. It was offered to me at a time when I could actually do it. My husband and I had gone our separate ways a few years back, and I was single, near retirement, in good health. I could safely describe myself as iconoclastic, so the personality fitted the task. Many in my family were pioneers of one sort or another. And I felt strongly that if my coming task could in some way prepare the path for my granddaughter, the effort would be well worth it.

I was further encouraged when information received via Billie from the otherworld checked out in this one. I knew that Billie had no personal knowledge of these matters.

For instance, I had been told that there was a major University "somewhere in the west of San Francisco" that would tell me very much about the faeries. This turned out to be quite true. It was the University of San Francisco, a Catholic institution. It has an extensive library selection of Gaelic faery lore, due to the large Celtic population it serves.

4

Another facility in California I was told of by Spirit was a relatively obscure rural spiritual centre in Escondido, California, called Questhaven. There "I would find angelic leaders dedicated to the nature spirits of all kinds who would be glad to assist me."

I located the centre, and found that the particular work of this retreat is the expression of Christian mysticism by learning through nature, by teaching, by expression of the creative arts and counselling. The study of the devic kingdoms is an essential part of the curriculum. These leaders did indeed help me, and totally validated my task. (2)

When you are ready, you are offered a challenge in your life. Like the Tarot Fool, you either stay on the edge or jump, even off a twig. I jumped.

Even though I made the jump, in the beginning I scrambled back up the tree many times. I was often a reluctant, belligerent adventurer at best. My rational mind still came upon me, and deluged me with darkness and doubt, much like the Irish showers I would soon become acquainted with. Yet, the sun would always come out.

It was time to make a commitment and move out on my own or to ignore the challenge. That would have been like ignoring a large elephant in the closet, and Spirit knew it!

Open that Door
Of Now and Before:

The Faery Host, Bringers of Light,
Behold them, Bestowers of the Sight!

II

Ireland at Last

Iarrived in Ireland on August 22, my birth date six decades before. From the moment I walked off the plane there was a sense of remembrance, an exultation, a delight in Ireland and the Irish. Even in gale force winds, or if my car has managed a flat tire in a rainstorm, even when I get my phone bill I have never been discouraged about Ireland. The winds lend themselves to a cosy fire; a country man invariably will stop to assist with the tire; an unexpected dividend will help fuel the finances.

One might suppose that a senior faery immigrant might have problems in relocating herself in a strange country. Problems there were, but finding a circle of friends was not one of them. From the very beginning this was so, in this gentle and hospitable land. This is not to deny that I have met those who have rejected my ways, but the normal stance is a sweet acceptance.

Initially in Dublin I contacted Minette, who was listed in one of my world-wide spiritual directories. With good humour and enthusiasm, she immediately came to my assistance. Minette and her practical husband Richard were just moving to County Carlow south of Dublin, where they had purchased a former rectory. It could accommodate themselves as well as guests beautifully, and they enthusiastically gave me a key to a room overlooking the courtyard.

Their garden is a fantasy of an Irish country garden, set naturally and profuse with lilies, roses, foxglove, honeysuckle, and delphiniums. Wild iris and their kin abound, and the vegetable garden is admirable.

It was so like my Grandmother Mullin's garden. She and her sister, both widows, lived on the outskirts of Bellingham, Washington; a half-day drive from our home in Seattle. It was an area characterised by tall conifers of many

6

descriptions, a myriad of clear lakes, cold winters and warm summers, and a definite country feeling.

My grandmother was short and plump and quite jolly and I admired her. Her sister Viola was a strikingly beautiful woman nearly six feet tall, a model and curator of the local museum, well into her eighties. Their house was full of crystal vases, antique plates, and lots of good and unusual smells like gingerbread and lavender.

Not far from the house there was a lake in which we children swam during our summer visits. As soon as we could get away we would be afoot on the sylvan trail that led to it through tall woods. A long sandy spit extended far out into the water, and the shallowness made swimming possible in the summer.

I remember so well the feel of the forest as I walked through it and the soft, delicate feel of the lake water, so much in contrast to the salty, buoyant water by our waterfront home on Puget Sound. The woodlands were full of wild violets, trilliums, and bluebells, not unlike the Irish woods I would traverse so many years later.

For reasons that are still obscure to me, during the middle years of my childhood I read the entire Bible twice, at least the verses that contained beautiful imagery. In the way of the Celt, I memorised a few of the poetic psalms and would recite them to the trees. I didn't know it then, but far away kin of mine were also reciting their favourite passages by glowing turf fires - and they would speak of the antics of the faeries at the same time!

He bowed the heavens also, and came down:
And darkness was under his feet.
And he rode upon a cherub, and did fly!
Yea, he did fly upon the wings of the wind.

Psalm 18

The easy, friendly way the Mullins lived was much like the ways of Irish friends I was meeting. Richard helped with me with the purchase of my 1982 Diahatsu, KK, named after her license plates. Richard doesn't take too much to the idea of faeries being about. Still, being a vintage motorcycle buff, if he were by chance to meet up with a little one on his excursions on the wild country roads, he wanted it to be "blasting away on a faery motorcycle, goggles, crash-helmet and all."

Nearly young enough to be my daughter, Minette took me under her wing like a mother hen, and through her I was introduced to several Dubliners with mutual interests.

I was finding that the faeries are just naturally accepted as a part of the Irish culture. Although some people feel it cosmopolitan to make light of this belief, there are many other urban dwellers of equal sophistication who have held on to the faith. They believe in the faery through contemporary eyes, incorporating the belief in a more esoteric, less fearful structure than did their predecessors. Resiliency is a characteristic of the faith.

The Irish sense of hospitality extended far beyond those of my immediate circle, and the courtesy of the rural people has perhaps to be experienced before it is believed. No matter how busy they might be, they have time for you. It is time given without thought of gain. This is the natural Celtic way.

Their sense of what is important is different from the priorities I have learned from the more materialistic culture I was acquainted with. One of the Celtic virtues is to recognise what is valuable in a spiritual sense and what is not. They realise that what I am doing is sincere and coming from the heart.

From the start I took my little tape recorder with me on interviews, and asked permission to record my conversations with those I met who were willing to talk to me about the faeries.

The stories I have collected from the people I met in Ireland are full of wisdom and humour. They reflect the culture and the courtesy of the people. It is a high culture, and, if I did not anticipate this immediately, it took me only a short time to realise it. That I have been fortunate enough to have conversed with holy men and women I do not doubt for a moment.

Minette accompanied me initially, and although this was helpful to me, I was to find that the presence of any third person added a complication to the process. It was enough for the Irish to cope with one "daft American", let alone her entourage.

My first interview: Minette and I were invited into the cobwebbed stone cottage of a gently decaying poet named Michael, who had been highly recommended by the bartender of the local pub as an expert on folk ways. The gatehouse residence consisted of three small rooms, all in a line facing an overgrown but perhaps once resplendent courtyard of an estate. The room to the right housed his motorcycle, the left room was his bedroom. We entered directly into the middle kitchen room, and although sparsely equipped it was very imaginatively appointed. Several different patterns of wallpaper adorned the walls, giving a harmonious collage effect; the ceiling and woodwork were painted in a variety of purple and lavender shades.

Michael entertained in his bedroom while he searched in his memory and his ancient battered suitcase for various poems to read us. Without a prompt, he referred to the faery and told us, amongst other stories, that his father often saw them dancing in the moonlight outside his home.

"My father, he'd look outside the window, and sometimes they'd be laughin' and sometimes cryin', they would. And then he'd know what kind of mood they were in."

He produced several "nearly finished" poems about the faery, about Ireland, about his emotional state. The later condition is perhaps best described by the two pictures he had on his wall. One was a pristine portrait of the Madonna, the other a calendar remnant of a bare-breasted Creole. As I thought he might be developing an eye for the ladies in the room, we escaped in Minette's mini car. Gales of laughter wafted us home that day!

My father Samuel never spoke of the faery that I can remember, but he was also a gentle poet like this man, a romantic. He was a journalist by trade and wrote stronger poetry, about the Armistice after the First World War, and the "troubles" of which he read so much about. Many books on Ireland lined his shelves.

It was by him that I was introduced at an early age to the works of the Irish writers. Those of a romantic persuasion were my choices, although he himself was more absorbed with political Ireland. William Butler Yeats and James Stephens were at once my favourites.

I have carried a copy of Stephen's classic book *The Crock of Gold* around with me all of my life. Still in print, it is definitely a highly recommended, magical, fey work of art. That Yeats also spoke so eloquently of the faery was not obvious to me until I engaged in this current research, nearly a half-century later. From Stephens:

> *"Come away! for the dance has begun lightly, the wind is sounding over the hill, the sun laughs down in the valley, and the sea leaps upon the shingle, panting for joy, dancing, dancing, dancing for joy..."* (3)

One of the reminiscences my father had about his retirement trips to Ireland was his fear of driving there. I faced this challenge immediately when arriving in Ireland, and had to learn how to drive on what I considered the wrong side of the road, and to use a gearstick to boot, as I had been advised by a mechanic that this would be my best buy. For many, it would be a change in habit readily adopted. For me, no.

I thought it logical that I start at the beginning, and so I took driving lessons while staying with Minette and Richard in County Carlow. It took more hours than I would care to mention before my red-haired driving instructor Frankie would feel comfortable in releasing me to the fates of the Irish road. At one point he asked me if I had ever had a heart attack, and when I answered no he said, "Well, there have certainly been times with you when I thought I was going to have one."

Frankie wasn't impressed with my mechanical aptitude but he was amused by my humour and was very glad that he survived the experience with his life and all limbs intact. He did say I improved, but to what degree he would not commit. Like a turtle learning ballet, perhaps.

My redhaired teacher's final remark to me about driving in Ireland was, "Remember two things, praise the good Lord and PLEASE stay between the two ditches." Frankie was not a man for abstractions. This was "concrete" advice.

No one would deny that it is a very prudent idea to literally stay between the ditches, for certain death is the usual alternative. It is also sensible to live under the Lord's protection while engaging the Donegal roads. When a milk truck comes at you going sixty miles an hour on a narrow country lane, there is little margin for error. It is necessary to be at peace. It steadies the hand.

The first hint I had that strange things often happen in Ireland was when my friends Sally and Ken Eyer and I visited an uninhabited castle somewhere in the Southeast of Ireland one sunny Sunday afternoon. They were over on a short visit with me from America, and we were sight-seeing. A place of historic interest, the castle was closed to visitors for the season and the gates were locked. The estate was situated on high ground, strategically placed against a rocky hillside for protection. It was in somewhat derelict condition, but quite handsome. It still clearly retained its exterior structure and some interior walls and floors, and had originally been three to four stories high.

As we were trespassing, we approached quietly, even though no one was in sight and there were no vehicles in the parking lot. He went to the right of the building, and I to the left. Coming up the meadow towards the castle, I distinctly heard three or four male voices coming from the second story.

The voices faded in and out as if their owners were walking around. One voice was deep, another lilting and light, the others less distinct. It was jovial and animated talk, in the way a group of construction workers in Ireland can be.

I guessed they were measuring the rooms for renovation. I couldn't make out any words, as their conversation was in the Gaelic I was beginning to recognise, interspersed with raucous laughter.

After a bit I called to Ken that we should take note of them in case they were cross with us for being there. He looked at me with puzzlement as he came towards me. "What men? What conversation?"

He hadn't heard a word of it. As he came to where I was standing, I ceased to hear the conversation. We investigated the castle and the grounds thoroughly, but no men, Irish or otherwise, could be found. When we returned to the car where Sally was resting, she said no one had come or gone. There was no other exit, only a cow trail up the hill.

I did hear that discussion. It was not the wind, nor faery music, nor my imagining. It wasn't even a flashy or significant event, but it did happen. Had I gone back in time for a moment, or had "they" come forward? Whatever happened, I was getting acquainted with a country that didn't have the same sets of rigid rules about time and space as other locations had.

I remember as a very young child I would try to convey to my mother that I saw grandma and her friend on the lawn swing talking, or the like, and she would laugh and say, "No, that hasn't happened yet. They are coming on the weekend." Or, "You couldn't have seen those people on the beach. They don't live here any more."

Yet, there I was again in perplexity. I did see these events, and even to my very young mind it seemed silly that I saw in this way. It wasn't even important, no one was angry, there were never misfortunes. I just saw grandma sitting on the lawn swing a few days too early - or a few years too late.

Neither my brother nor I did much talking until we were four. My guess on this is that we didn't need to talk. Not knowing that it was thought unusual, I would communicate with my brother by simply focusing my attention on what I wanted to convey. Our baffling conspiracy was eventually broken up by those who felt it prudent for us to come out of our "cone of silence".

I had enunciation lessons at an early age, and am still accused of speaking like a shadow. My brother's nickname was "mumbles Mullin", and he solved his particular dilemma by becoming a speech professor.

III

Going Around in Circles

Sometimes we go
    when the wind blows
And sometimes we go
    and only God knows
Or when it snows...

Returning with the rain
Then off again...
Coming and going
Reaping and sowing.

Sometimes east
Sometimes west:
Round and round and round is best!

Humour was everywhere, I was finding. The Wicklow Way is a nature trail originating in Dublin that winds through the Wicklow mountain area, ending up in the enchanted village of Clonegal that is about 40 km south of the capital city. The travel brochures all mention it, but finding an actual map of the walk is difficult. Most likely you won't be able to find one unless you go into Dublin, and if you are lucky you might find one there.

A long wilderness walk appealed ever since I first read of the Way in my travel book. I wanted to keep up on my exercise regimen, and had it in mind to "get into nature". My problems began when I decided to start out on this two day adventure beginning at Clonegal, the technical end of the walk. This termination point was only a short distance from where I was staying, and Dublin was two hours travel by car.

I reasoned that walking one way on a route is essentially the same way as walking the other way. So I asked the owner of the pub, the gas station, and the grocery store in Clonegal where the trail started.

"Dublin."

"Where does it end?" I queried.

"It's down the road a piece," was the answer.

I asked him if the trail went all the way to Dublin, and he looked at me and nodded. My valiant chauffeur Minette and I went in the indicated direction, but could not find the trail markers he said were there. We stopped at the roadside about three miles down and asked a farmer where the trail started. He said, "Well, you'd have to be goin' back to Clonegal if you're to be startin' where the trail ends."

There are such fixed routes all over Ireland (and most likely everywhere else). One way is the right way, the opposite direction is the wrong way. Someone suggested these rules came about because the trails were old cow paths, and the "cows only come home one way". Another was adamant that some trails were "former faery paths", and that "you simply never interfere with anything they have done". Whether the faeries would agree in this case, I don't know.

The farmer finally agreed to tell us where the "trail" left the road to enter the forest preserve, and we eventually found our marker. Minette drove away, and off I went with my backpack and American vanity to walk the six mile journey to Shillelagh and to stay overnight at a hostel, just as the guide books suggested. Six miles, I can do that in a wink. I'll be there easily in time to meditate in the virgin woods and venture to the pubs in search of my stories.

I followed the markers and followed the markers and eventually realised I was going around in circles. They were wonderful circles, full of gorgeous farmland vistas, forest walks, mossy glens, wild flowers, and a wonderful stillness. But circles, nonetheless. I kept ending up with some minor variations in exactly the same spot I entered. It eventually came to me that I was simply going around the top of a mountain - the same mountain.

I finally exited at the suggestion of a marker but had to climb a locked gateway to get to the road. After a late morning and afternoon of walking, I arrived approximately one quarter mile from where I started.

Only my faery guides could have led me straight to an impressive farmhouse Bed and Breakfast - the only accommodation within 10 miles in that scarcely populated area. At each crossroads I had made the correct decision on which way to go.

I inquired about the problem of the walk with proprietors Bridget and Seamus. They were quite aware of difficulties, because other hikers had also expressed frustration. Seamus admitted that no one has found the trail from Shillelagh to the next indicator on the Wicklow Way. Things will be better next year, they both maintained. Of course, the reason no one has found the trail is because there isn't one, but I did not directly suggest that to them.

Bridget did say that I was close enough now to Shillelagh to pick up the trail north to Dublin. She carefully told me where I could enter. In the morning I followed her directions, and this time I realised sooner that I was again going round and round a mountain. It was a different mountain, a little closer to the Way, but it was still not connected to any trail.

As the sun settled in the western sky, I started downhill. Soon it would be dusk. The path came to an abrupt end at the beginning of a field. I was faced with traversing a moat or retreat, which meant going back uphill about a mile. I decided to attempt the moat. First, I crawled through a sheep sized opening to a field that led downwards, then traversed a steep culvert that separated the first field from the one next to the road.

To get to the road I had to climb over a high fence barricaded by blackberry vines and thistles. I found a tree with a beckoning lowlying branch and propelled myself onto the top, bypassing the barbed wire. On the other side a ditch separated the fence from the road and was easily a five foot drop. I grabbed another stalwart branch and swung down and crash landed in a combination of nettles, grass and a few berry branches.

If I ever needed a faery person, it was on the way back from my walk. I had journeyed at least twelve miles, and my feet were not wishing to be connected to me any longer. Then I saw a woman walking on the road. She was matronly and comfortable in appearance with her apron and printed skirt and shawl, typical Irish farm dress for a previous generation. Peculiar place for the likes of her though, as farm women do not, as a rule, stroll by themselves along the road.

16

I approached her eagerly, believing she could have a solution to my dilemma. She greeted me with, "Now isn't it grand you be out by yourself, takin' care of yourself like you do".

I was surprised because I would draw no such attention in America, but I suppose I did look a novelty to her, with my backpack, sturdy shoes, slacks, and set jaw. In Ireland women my age never wear slacks, and they certainly would never carry a backpack or go hiking if they could avoid it. She repeated her genuine compliment again, exclaiming how wonderful it was that I was self sufficient and out on the roads by myself. It was a loving statement from a warm and caring mother, although we were probably pretty close to the same age.

I asked if this was the way to Clonegal and she said, "Well, isn't it wonderful for me to be here now, so I can be tellin' you that you're goin' the wrong way. Isn't it grand I can be tellin' you! Cause otherwise you'd be goin' up this road and it would be doin' you no good at all. This road don't be goin' anywhere, and you don't want to be on this one. You be turnin' around and go back a piece to the crossroads. Turn right and you'll be on your way. Bless you, you bein' takin' care of yourself."

I thanked her and went on my way. Once I looked back and she waved to me and when I looked again she was gone. Maybe she lived in the farmhouse down the road. Maybe she just disappeared, like a faery guide. She was sweet and gentle, and her eyes were full of humour and mischief. The lovely lady was truly happy for me, and there was as much joy in it for her, as if she had greeted a friend of long acquaintance.

Nettles and ferns point the Way
Shall I go on or shall I stay?
The road bends
But never ends...

My maternal Grandma Sprague, the one I occasionally saw sitting on the lawn swing when she wasn't quite there yet, had this caring manner so characteristic of older Irish women. I adored her. I thought she was exceptionally beautiful, even in old age, and her photographs attest to a delicate youthful loveliness. Grandma was saddened with life when I knew her, but she was never depressive, never cross with me, always present. She was an experience of unconditional love. No matter what I said or felt, she understood.

Grandma lived in a small flat in the middle of Seattle, and earned her living as a dressmaker almost until she died in her seventies. Her family emigrated from Ireland, arriving in Canada. She married and gave birth to several children, but none survived except my mother. Grandma came across the great plains in a covered wagon, suffering the terror of Indian raids and living the rugged, demanding life of a plains woman. She was once well-to-do, but her fortune had been dissipated by her late, gambling husband.

When I visited her, I would sleep on a cot she would pull down from the wall. She would fry potatoes in a greasy pan. At night she would tuck me in and I would find all kinds of coins she had saved for me from her hard-working days, and she would talk to me. There was no radio, no television, no distractions for a small slip of a child with unruly red hair, but I was never bored, never uncomfortable with her.

I wanted to build her a castle with a big, green lawn running down to the sea. There would be all sorts of flowers about, as she loved them in particular. I would come and visit her every day and play the harp for her, so that she would never be lonely.

While I was at the B&B, proprietor Bridget introduced me to a young American woman who was also staying there for a short while. Being of Irish descent, she had an immediate sense of my project, and was instrumental in guiding me to the Dingle peninsula in the Southwest. "There is a man who runs a B&B there, you'd do well to meet him. I think he is a mystic, as his family has been in the area for 1,000 years." She gave me his card, and my car KK and I were soon on our way.

It was no task to find the Dingle peninsula or the mystic's farm, as everyone for miles knew who Ted, the owner, was. The farmhouse was a sturdy, whitewashed large dwelling that housed not only the summer visitors but Ted's large and lovely family as well. Settled high on a hill, it overlooks a beautiful white strand. The location has not suffered from any signs of intruding civilisation. It looks much as it might have looked long, long ago.

I expected to find someone somewhat obscure, but when I met Ted my impression was corrected. Tall, lean and looking quite a bit like an Irish version of Gary Cooper, Ted greeted me with bold enthusiasm. I was astonished when I walked into the den and found a library full of metaphysical books, and a copy of the latest channelled book from America on the table in plain sight. A fellow student, a fellow seeker, living in a homestead 1,000 years old! We talked for hours - about the second sight, the obscure, the intangible.

I found Ted to be a firm believer in the little ones and the unseen worlds. This is how he spoke of it to me:

"It is just something that comes into your mind without you really thinking about it. Even yourself there, now. When I first saw you I had the feeling that I had met you before. The explanation I can get for that one is that I probably met you in what the aborigines would call the Dreamtime, in the astral, because everything that has happened, everything that is happening now, and everything that will happen in the future has already happened in the fourth dimension.

"A part of us lives in the fourth dimension - the higher self - from where we get our personality patterns. We don't remember, because of the denseness of this world. The separation has already ended. We actually are Gods right now. We actually are divine. If you really think about it, it stands to reason. Fear is the enemy because it is defensive in nature."

He went on to tell me how many in that area had seen or sensed the presence of faery. This picturesque story is about his grandfather:

"I remember one time we were at the races at the strand - there were local horses racing on the beach. There would be drink, and all the old ones would head for it straight away, and meet up with people and relations they hadn't seen for maybe a year. And they'd all come and chat. I remember my grandfather being there, and he would be fairly steamed up. The boys knew how to get him going, you know. They'd get him to talk about his faeries. So he was telling about coming home one night, and inside the ditch, he was telling how he was staring at a faery. That was the gist of it. I remember him getting angry about it because they were really playing with him. I started to laugh myself because he was so, you know, so upset himself.

"Later in life I found out that so many of us were psychic, grandfather especially. People thought grandfather was a bit foolish, but he wasn't, it was just that those things really happened to him."

Ted went on to talk of many mystical experiences in his family, a natural, integrated part of their way of being. It was easy to tell him of an experience I had that I was shy in talking about with anyone else.

At one time in my graduate student career we were studying Eastern mysticism. Much of it was quite foreign to me, and I found it difficult but challenging. One semester we spent time with an Indian trained in meditation, and, on occasion, would go to his ashram in San Francisco, California.

A few days after one such all-day intensive, I had what I would have to call a "vision". I was alone that particular night, and had fallen asleep in my bed while reading. I awoke later with a start, and was immediately apprehensive. The room was ice cold, unusual in that area during the warm season. I felt the bed covers and the paper I was reading, and reached to turn on the light, but it did not respond even though I had recently installed a new light bulb.

I was wide awake. Without reason the room became even colder and suddenly a giant, multi-plumed bird-like creature "appeared" at the end of my bed. It resembled an ostrich to some extent, but that is a pale comparison. It was the first time in my life that I was literally scared stiff. I couldn't move a muscle.

Then, to the left, a blonde woman in a long white dress appeared. She had an expression of serene power and held a blazing emblem in her hand, which I would identify later as a Celtic cross. She looked slightly annoyed at the bird as if it were a misbehaving pet, and banished it summarily. She regarded me kindly but firmly and conveyed to me that she was a member of the "Sisterhood of Light". The room became warm and luminous, and my fear faded. She then communicated that I, too, was a member of the sisterhood. Anytime that I would "come" to where she was, she would be there. Specifically she said, "I will be with you always, even until the end of being."

Then she simply and quietly vanished and somehow I fell into the most peaceful sleep I had ever known. I woke up at dawn. Ted listened intently to my story, but he wasn't particularly surprised. Similar things had happened in his family.

It was on his suggestion that I visited the remotest village I had ever been in, in search of a holy well that was located there. Almost hidden in the hills behind Ventry, the village proved well worth the trials KK had winding up the rocky road to it. "St. Bridget's Well" is linked to an early Milesian invasion that took place on the White Strand beach about a mile away. The story goes that there was a large flat stone placed adjacent to the mainspring of the well after the battle. It was removed some time ago to be used as a cornerstone in a building,

but it apparently did not like its new location, and found the way back home on its own. It had also cracked in two on the return journey, perhaps to ensure its rightful place at the well.

I was to contact a Mr. Murphy, who owned the "farmhouse with the new red roof". A small, sturdily built woman who was working in her garden directed me to the Murphy residence with enthusiasm. I met the "Missus", but Mr. Murphy was "not about" that morning. She said that if I wanted to find out about the well and the moving stones I had best talk to Mr. Shea, who had "lived next to it his whole life - he ought to know something about it!"

It turned out that Mr. Shea was not about either that morning, but Mrs. Shea was pleased to be interviewed. I told her I was looking for the well with the moving stones, "St. Bridget's, I believe".

"The Lord himself turned water into wine, turned water into wine," she said without missing a beat, "and on the day he did it, which was the twenty ninth of June, there were three here at this well, on that same day. They turned the water into wine, but it was magic how they did it. They weren't supposed to tell, so when they all looked back they turned into stone. That's why those three stones used to be there."

There weren't any stones, and admittedly the story got a little fragmented, but it was delivered with style and conviction. There was a rectangular rock at the base of the well that had been severed in two in the middle, and on the stone's surface a smaller ornamental rectangle had been carved. It could have been a cornerstone.

There was also another rock with a handsome Celtic cross carved on the surface. Mrs. Shea said that usually when tourists come looking, they would go down the field to another well. "That is not the real one", she explained sweetly. I was shown the authentic one because I was Irish and not one of "those others".

She said that on that date in June all the villagers come and rub their eyes with water from the well, and become cured of any eye difficulties. I didn't see anyone with glasses on, it is true. But then I only saw Mrs. Murphy and Mrs. Shea.

Many of my Irish friends had suggested that Connemara would be a fitting place to continue my search. It is more northerly and isolated than the Dingle peninsula, and one of the few remaining locations in Ireland that is known for its efforts to preserve the Irish language and culture. It is a particularly rugged, windswept part of the western coastline of Ireland, having far less arable land than other areas. "A poor pile of rocks and bog, it is. It is undesirable for farming, true."

Some of my most genuine stories were collected in the byway areas of Connemara, and I scarcely touched the surface. If a country person did not have faery awareness, almost all of them remembered the old ones talking about it. Although there were some scoffers, they were in the minority here. I was to find that this pattern consistently held throughout the west of Ireland.

On my first night in Roundstone, a fishing village on the southern coast, I met some hearty seafaring men while "pubcrawling". I was trying to do the challenging assignment suggested by Spirit, to actually go into a pub by myself and engross the occupants in conversation.

Ryan's Bar was my choice, as that is where I was told the locals hang out. Hardy turf fires warmed and lit the dark room somewhat, and it smelled slightly dank and seaworthy, as if you were inside a trawler, or in the belly of Jonah's whale. Its charm lay in its honesty, and no tourist would be likely to tarry here. Even though it was facing on the beautiful bay, the kitchen blocked any view of the harbour. Those who came in there to drink and meet had enough of the sea, they wanted to be out of sight of the cold.

There were three men at the other end of the bar who were getting drunk with great enthusiasm and conviction when I slipped in at 7:30 p.m. These locals were talking about what men usually talk about everywhere, business, weather, sports, and the events of the day. They knew I was there because I was an oddity, but were only paying peripheral attention to me. Then, the dark skinned blackhaired younger man in the middle asked me where I was from. His name was Danny.

"California."

"Are they still goldmining in California, and if we were to go there would we find some gold?" Danny queried.

"No, but you have gold in your hearts," I said, but they all ignored the remark.

"There is gold in the Connemara hills, but it can't be mined for they would be disturbing a faery rath or a site some sort like that," added the stocking-capped man called Tim who was seated closest to me.

Then to my amazement, even though their thick brogue and the mixture of Gaelic phrases with English made eavesdropping difficult, they started talking about local ghosts and haunted houses.

"I do not believe in haunted houses, it is all a tourist trick," said Seamus, who was resolutely sitting at the end of the bar. He told his friends this with a very authoritative voice. Portly and ruddyfaced, he was cleanly attired in a hand-woven tweed jacket and an Irish cap.

Middle man Danny was in disagreement with Seamus, and went on to tell several stories in succession about haunted and ghost houses he had visited. Much of his conversation was inaudible. My recorder picked up strands of it, and my Irish friends have filled in. It went something like this:

"My mother was tendin' the farm... and then she got very sick, and she was on the bed to die. And my sister was goin' out on the path, down to get some turf there. And she saw the father who was dead. She got a fright, she got a shock, she did.

"She died the same night, my mother. And so he was waitin' for her, he was. The father was waitin', you see.

"I heard him tell a lot of ghost stories. Now I remember him tellin' me about it. He was comin' home from shoppin' on his bicycle. He saw this wee woman, but he thought she was goin' to a house which was right there. And he saw her passin' another man, this man was a hunchback. And when she got close to him he says, 'Who are you, and where are you goin'? My father said that.

"But the woman just cut away and she just floated over the briars. Away off. So then he knew it was a ghost."

"He went up to the man and he says, 'Who was she, that woman?

"'I saw no woman, ' the hunchback said.

"She was covered from head to the toes in white. White, Aye."

Tim was engrossed in an inner dialogue, half-relating to his friends some occurrence of his that he could not explain, but it could have been a ghost.

"They used to see people who had passed on and were lost souls. Mass was said for the souls. That's puttin' them at ease. This was before my time, after the

persecution. They want the people to know they have left this world. That's why they come back. They don't interfere with anyone," Tim said.

"If my father saw some dead person that he knew, he wouldn't want to say who it was, like. I think most people would be like that anyway. They wouldn't want to blame anyone," Danny explained. The others nodded in agreement.

"In the harbour there is this story," Tim continued. "There was a man there one night waiting for the change in tide with his father and he saw this boat approaching the harbour in the moonlight. So the father told the son to go down and have a jug of poteen (home-brew), but don't drop the keg. They will be cold when they come ashore! And on his way the son slipped on the turf and fell between the keel and a hole and was drowned. (Long pause) And there was no boat, no boat."

Then surprisingly the subject shifted to the topic of faeries. Seamus, the florid disbeliever in ghosts, was first to comment.

"Some people say they are seen," pointing his hand as if he were describing a bird in flight, "goin' this way and that way, but I don't believe that. I don't believe in them meself. I never saw one. I don't believe in them at all."

"People used to see them too, with the ghosts," added Danny. "I didn't see them, or my parents didn't, but people did, you know. They are dead and gone, those people who used to see."

"The only thing I ever heard about the faeries was an old man from around here was up one night very late," Tim added. "He went out to the field behind his house and he saw a lot of faeries dressed in red coats and marching round the field beating on tin cans as if they were drums."

Danny was again in some kind of debate about the statement. He was fairly neutral on the idea. At this point they did take note of my curiosity, even though I hadn't changed my expression.

"I do want to know the truth about the faeries, I'm really here doing research on folklore..."

"Maybe what would be best for you would be a Connemara man and not a faery," Tim suggested.

This caused Danny to giggle almost uncontrollably. Such an outspoken sexual statement I found to be very, very rare among the Irish, even to a woman alone at the bar, whatever they might be thinking.

I left shortly after, as I thought the Connemara man named Danny might soon fall off his barstool and I didn't want to be a contributing cause. He might well be more amusing to be with than a faery, but not under the existing conditions.

It was truly wondrous to find a group of hearty, earthy working men talking seriously about the subject of ghosts and faeries with as much dedication as they had when discussing football scores. With not a hint of embarrassment. It was truly what Spirit had told me would happen, almost a year ago and halfway around the globe.

When my father visited Ireland after his retirement, he used to love to go into the pubs, to talk with the Irish and play darts. He was as much of a ham as any of them ever thought of being.

I never "saw" him after he died, but Shirley, a friend of my mother's, claimed she did. Shirley was a freckled Irish one with bright, almost orange hair. I thought her a bit crazy, but I believed her story because of her two poodles.

"It was like this, Kay. I was sitting with your mother Dorothy, out in the back patio, early evening. Maybe a month or so after your father died. She had gone in to tend some chores, and I walked with the dogs clear to the creek. Suddenly, they started barking hysterically, and were terribly frightened. I looked towards the house, and we were about thirty feet away. There, right by the back door I saw your father. Clearly. He didn't look at me, he was just standing. For a moment or two, and then he just went away. Dorothy wasn't there, nor did she see him. The poodles were still so scared they were rigid. Ask her, she saw them when she came out. We had to put them in the car."

IV

The Road to Donegal

As the chill winds of the Irish November of 1991 greeted me with boldness, I returned to California with reluctance. By then I was convinced of the presence of faery, or at least the presence of something very gentle, very challenging that was still happening on the western shores of Ireland.

Doubt came and went, but I knew I would be back the following spring, and the road pointed to Donegal. "If you want to be hearin' the best stories about the faeries, then it's Donegal where you should go. That's the best county for that. The reason is, it is cut off, you know. Yes, that is still Ireland."

Another said very similarly, "If you would spend time in the really remote hills of Donegal, where the people still live as they did maybe a century ago, there is where you would still find your stories about the faeries and the great ones of the past. They are living as their grandparents did."

My initial short stay in Donegal, in the spring of 1992 was in a cabin perched high on a hill close to Malin Head, the very northern tip of Ireland. There was a narrow driveway to the side of the house, and a long concrete stairway stood right beside it.

The first day I was there I distinguished myself to my rather stuffy English landlord by backing KK - not down the narrow driveway - but onto the concrete steps on the first and only trial. It would be hard for a stunt driver to imitate this task even if he ever wanted to. It took two strong neighbour men to lift KK off her imprisoned perch. I was properly flustered, and further dignified myself by driving away down the wrong side on a bend of a winding road.

This house, however, was not to be my abode for long. Soon after, I rented an Irish cottage that was close to the town of Ardara in western Donegal. This name kept popping into my head, and when I located it on the map I went there straight away. By asking around and looking at the bulletin boards, I located my cottage with ease. It was the only suitable one, my landlady had "just put the notice up," and the place would be vacant all summer.

It is curious. For a long time I had an "idea" in my head about what my cottage would look like. The wee house closely matched the idea - like something you recall - even the orientation and the location of the stream. Simply structured, it had a small living room with a turf-lit fire that fuelled the central heating, an efficient kitchen, two small bedrooms and a bath.

It was right by the sea, a bonny place and not too dear, with a promontory view of the everchanging bay of Gweebarra. Sometimes the waters are sombre and turbulent, but on a quiet day the tides create a stillness that allows the farmhouses on the northerly side to clearly reflect their pristine beauty. To witness a red sunset is breathtaking. Even the locals - livestock and people - stop their daily tasks to gaze at the wonders of Gweebarra.

Many summer adventures presented themselves. One opportune day I went to the coastal village of Glencolumbkille[1], a short distance from Ardara. Its fog shrouded valleys were once the home of Columba of Iona, where there is little doubt he set up a monastery.

Classes in the Irish language, customs, and heritage are given there throughout the summer months, and I chose a lecture on the 14th and 15th century architecture. To my surprise, from my reading of faery history I knew quite a bit of what the Professor was talking about. [4]

A purpose of the lecture was to give information on the area's historical sites for those who were to perform the "walk" later in the day. It was June 9, Saint Colm Cille's Day. Traditionally there is a lengthy pilgrimage around fifteen cross slabs and pillars known as The Stations of the Cross. The stalwart clerics of old did this journey of penitence on a regular basis. It took our group of twelve nearly five hours to perform the stations. We covered about five miles of vertical mountain ground, and waded through marshes one could swim in. The leader, a beatific, barefooted, bald man scurried up the hills like a mountain goat and through the bogs with the agility of a frightened hare. Reverent, joyful, humourous it was - and wet.

It was clammy and cold that evening. My fellow penitents and I arrived at the local pub without delay, our demeanour and purpose changed. A lively local gent, on hearing of our adventures, admitted that he also did his "stations" on a regular basis. However, he performed this ancient ritual at midnight so that no one could see him - in the manner that the true and innocent repentants actually did. His purpose "would therefore be pure". This speech was given with the practised Irish straight face, and his humour certainly met its mark. The only other woman in our group, a non-local like myself, believed him.

One day I was working on the book when Mary, my landlady, came to pick up something from the garage. I had just turned the computer on for the day when she came, and it was quite apparent that something was wrong with it. I envisioned all sorts of tragedies that I heard of but knew almost nothing about. Alas, who could help me? I did not think that anyone around here could be of any assistance. Would this be The End?

I mentioned to Mary that my computer wasn't working, but it was more of an aside remark, as she knew nothing about "those kind of machines". She said "not to worry, because she knew a local computer expert who had recently retired from an electronic firm in England due to back problems and "he'd come right over".

Well, he did come over within the hour and he was an expert, retired from IBM. The problem was due to the electrical eccentricities of Donegal power, and could be coped with. He also fixed some wiring that was defective, so his visit was more than welcomed.

If you have ever been to Dear Old Donegal you might wonder if a computer expert had ever visited here. You would certainly not expect to find one, not in this wild and green land. Why would a computer expert come here to live? I probably had one of the few home computers in all of western Donegal. Yet, there he was. Only a mile down the road, there for all time for my assistance if I need it. He also told me where to get my materials printed. And where to dig for cockles, where to pick mussels, and how to approach the fishermen for fresh salmon and oysters.

Further, being a curious and lively fellow, he asked me what I was writing about. I told him briefly, and he thought it a fine idea. He gave me the names of several people in the area who would be excellent prospects for interviews - the old people, of course.

"They have what they call their 'quiet places' around here - those places where you might find the sort of thing you are talking about. I'm a logical man myself, but there has to be something to all those beliefs, the second sight they call it, too. More to it than we know."

Surprisingly, he recommended most highly the local expert in folklore: Mary's father, Paddy. So, I found a treasure nearly under my own roof, my landlady's father. It would seem that indeed I was being helped.

One facet of Irish country culture that I was initially and naively unaware of was the level of community awareness. Everyone knew where everyone lived and what they did, and most likely knew what their kin had been up to for generations. When friends from northern Donegal came to visit me one day, they weren't sure of directions and so stopped at a house a mile or so down the road to inquire of the whereabouts of "the American lady". The occupants, whom I had never met, told my friends exactly where I lived. Further:

"Her mother is from Carmel, California, and is visiting her for a month, and she is almost ninety. And Clint Eastwood's mother lives right next door to the mother."

In America, mothers are often thought of in the past tense, and rarely determine overtly the activities of their middle-aged children. But in these rural communities they are not only omnipresent, but have considerable status. My mother was treated like a celebrity, and took every advantage of it. Not only is she still agile mentally, but she is physically strong and has young ideas.

One day, early in my stay in Ardara, I was taking a walk on my mountain road - a very private loop used almost entirely by the residents who live on it. I was ambling down to the main road about a mile away, where I turned around and returned. At the crest of the hill a local man of middling age was attending his cows. He was as sturdy as his fourlegged companions, and surveyed me as carefully as one might an animal at a country fair. We exchanged pleasantries, and although his brogue was nearly unintelligible I gathered he was welcoming the "Yank".

He was still there when I came back on that stretch of the road a little while later. This time he was more adamant in getting his message through, and asked me quite pointedly, "Are ye married?"

Frustrated by his inability to decipher my musings about matrimony, I finally distinctly said, "No."

Again he scanned me thoroughly, and said, "Well, have ye thought on it?" He then shook my hand, perhaps to seal some inner bargain he knew of but I didn't.

I often saw the Mountain Man after that, but waved and walked on by. He was one of five brothers living with "the mother", and I would occasionally give them rides to the bog. They were protective of "the Yank" if others were present, but he himself did not pursue his query any further.

Perhaps my momentary suitor was like a typical Irish bachelor, described by the wit from Belfast, who was later to come into my life:

"There was the typical Irish bachelor son, about 45. He lived at home with the mother and father. The mother died, leaving him and his eighty year old father to tend the house. It became a joint decision that they needed a woman about the house.

"The son went out to look for a wife, and there were a few the father didn't like. However, the son found one he was keen on. He told this to the father after he brought her home for the first time.

"Well, dad, what do you think of her?" he queried.

"We will discuss business at the pub," was the father's reply. So they went to the place where such matters are discussed.

"Well, you've seen her. I like her. Will she do?" the son said hopefully.

"Well, she's a good looking girl, and she might do. But how would she look between two buckets of pig feed?"

I myself might not look so good between two buckets, but I was learning some Irish ways. It is said here that one should go no further than the dung heap to find a mate, and there is likely great wisdom in that.

On the dunghill the cock crows,
Men, women and children awake:
But faeries never sleep, God knows
And are as clear-eyed as a morning lake!

V

Pádraic's Name

The language of the Gael, that I am attempting haphazardly to learn, is rich and fascinating, as even a cursory study will reveal. It is spiritually abundant in its thinking, having many words that describe specific metaphysical experiences. It is also one of the most bawdy of languages, having a wide range of words for various types of personal noises usually thought to be embarrassing. Reverent, irreverent. Religious, sacrilegious.

When throwing out your pail of water
On a morning bright and airy:
Always say "Seachain! Beware!"
In case you'd drown a faery!

A particularly melodious Irish word, *imram*[2], designates the act of rowing or a voyage to the otherworld. If you want to sail across the great Irish sea to *Tír na nÓg*, the land of eternal youth, you find yourself a coracle and so voyage. Many did, and they were never seen again in this world.

Up the lane a bit from my Gweebarra cottage there is a little lake beyond the glen, where two white swans have their abode. A mile beyond that a wee Irish cottage rests in the hill, oblivious to any modern convenience. The scene is completely hidden from view from all but the lucky hiker, who is able to view sacred Ireland traversing these hidden places. One evening I was walking up there at sunset. The reeds in the lake cast their shadows so perfectly you couldn't tell where the reeds ended and where their images began. One could not tell which sunset was the real one, the one in the sky or the one in the lake.

There was no sound except that of the brook cascading down the hill and the bleating of the lambs who were distressed at such a peculiar and intrusive sight as I. For a while, a long while actually, I had no sense of myself, and yet I was thoroughly grounded. Then, when I recovered from this state, I knew it was then that I would have found my *imram* - vessel, carved out of a single log, with one fine oar. It would surely have taken me to faeryland.

As I reached the crest of the hill the sun was slipping beneath the waters of the western sky. The symphony of apple and fuchsia-red hues filled the world there, and one could see forever.

When the Light is draining from the sky
It's then They leap, it's then They fly
Until subdued by the milky moon
Under a hawthorn in a swoon.

Dusk was just beginning to suggest itself when I called upon Pádraic one day. His cottage settled comfortably into the hillside along the mountain road between Glenties and Ballybofey, part of the landscape of many seasons. The front hallway typically centred the house, dividing it somewhat in two. After his lady surveyed me and decided to let me in, I met Pádraic in the small living room. The chairs were placed around the turf-burning stove, in much the same fashion as in my wee cottage.

He was expecting me, as I had made an appointment. His initial greeting was one of gladness, a look I had come to appreciate with the country people I was privileged to interview. He remained the whole time in his chair. Perhaps he simply wished to, or his 80 some years and fierce mountain winds had given him a not uncommon stiffness of the joints.

I explained my mission as simply as I could, omitting any credential or purpose except to say that I was of Irish descent and interested in what he had to say. He had been recommended by the locals as a man who was knowledgeable of the Irish ways.

There was scarcely a prompt of any sort, but Pádraic was soon onto the faery stories. I had in no way told him those would be a main interest of mine. Rather, it was what he wanted to talk about that day.

He told me about a "faeryman" who came to his area as a mysterious stranger and hardly ever smiled or spoke to anyone. "Kept to himself, he did."

Yet this enigmatic one ended up being the local hero. With only the help of his faery "posse" he thwarted a cattle raid which had been instigated by the lowlanders. In what must have been a spectacular sight, the stolen cattle were rounded up and returned safely home on the very road I had just travelled. In his grandfather's time, that is when it happened.

Pádraic told me of the mountain behind the lake that received its name from that event. I had passed it on my way here.

I learned about music that "was heard", and of the faery camps that were seen on top of the hill behind his house on special fair days. They would disappear when the curious climbed to investigate! I heard about the man who suddenly got the gift of healing and foretelling when he slept out in the bog one night.

"Drunk he was, and so he slept out in that field across there and slept on a book and after that he could read the book and foretell, even though he didn't know how to read. Isn't that something?" He went on to tell me about all the predictions of this man that came true over the years.

I heard a story about his father who had a dream in which an angel appeared and called out Pádraic's name. His father took it as a sign and kept Pádraic home that day to protect him from harm. So, Pádraic did not go on a venture that nearly cost the lives of his young companions who were allowed to go. Had the angel visited their house, they too would have been detained. Had he gone,

Pádraic might not have survived the fastmoving, swollen river, as he was the youngest of the lot. "Isn't that something?"

When I explained that I lived in a cottage much like theirs, and stoked my peat stove in the same way that they did, Pádraic's wife became noticeably more accepting of me. She told me of a house that was "haunted by the faeries" close to where I lived. I knew of the very house. Close to the Gweebarra strand, derelict for years, it had recently been renovated to accommodate the tourist trade which was looked on with ambivalence by the locals.

"There were faeries there all right, they could hear them singin' and dancin' from the second story. There was talk about that. That's after it was deserted. But it's too crowded now there by the beach. The faeries have gone away."

She then looked at me speculatively, but it was clear I was not going to laugh or make jest of her. I believed every word she said. I would indeed be honoured to live in a house that is haunted by the faeries, even if their revelries kept me awake all night long. I would be joyfully delighted, and join them if they would let me.

Hush a bye hush
The faery croon,
All is quiet
From here to the moon:
Though your eyes are open, you are asleep
Field-mice cavort in the shadows deep:
Hush a bye Hush, shoheen shoh-hoh,
The faery croon so sweet and low!

Between Pádraic's home and that of another mountain person I was calling on, there is a long stretch of the road, maybe five miles, where there are no inhabitable dwellings. Only scrubby pasture lands, bogs and sheep greet the lonesome car. Locals do not like to travel there. The road hugs the mountain and that evening the fog lay upon the valley floor in individual patches, like clouds. I stopped at a crossroads where a nearly vanished stone dwelling once housed a large family. The valley by full moon looked as if it could have been a sky world within itself. No lights or other marks of civilisation defined it, and it seemed to have no particular boundaries. Down the hill was the lake where the silent stranger had met with his group of faeries and intercepted the cattle raid.

"It was a long time ago this happened," Pádraic had said. It was in his grandfather's time, and his grandfather talked about it all his life. "Oh, this country was strange in those days. It was strange. Don't you think so?"

I had been to the places he was talking about, and had met a few of the people who belonged there, in that moonscape. They had lived their lives there, with their loves and with their dreams. Pádraic himself was born in his house, and had lived there for nearly 90 years. All this time he held on to these stories of the supernatural. They were not stories to him, they were real events. He knew that life is a mystery, that the ineffable is at our fingertips if we live in a place of mist, of gentleness, of moon meadows.

It is said of the mountain people that they have a hard time distinguishing between reality and the supernatural, but the truth is they distinguish quite well. The supernatural is their reality, and they are holding onto it because it has meaning in their lives. It is a land where the faeries do dance in the meadow and the ghosts walk at midnight.

I had also been told that they put on a show for the gullible, and don't believe their own yarns. To me it seems, however, that after some practice it is not that hard to tell the difference between what they believe in and what gets embroidered in a story. Pádraic believed in the faeries, and in foretelling, and the music of the meadow. He particularly held to be true the shining angel who visited his father in a dream and softly called out his name.

Within a month after I visited Pádraic he died quietly. It was not in his own cosy bed in his whitewashed mountain abode, but in a sterile hospital room with crisp, unfamiliar white sheets to cover him. Did he hear the angel call out again, "Pádraic, Pádraic"?

As a child, I had noticed angels about. Just that. These incredibly beautiful forms of luminosity were in the sky for the main part. They were not always present, but were visible especially when the sunlight came through the clouds in a particular way. I did not question their authenticity, nor did it occur to me that perhaps not everyone saw them. They seemed so natural, and yet it was hard to put this into words.

Some sort of recurring dream about my guardian angel would come to me, too. A luminous, feminine form, with a distinctly clear voice. I remember her telling me simply but firmly that I must choose between right and wrong - the right way would not always appear as easy as the wrong one, but it was the way to go. Then she would show me two paths. One looked more tempting than the other, as it ambled downwards as opposed to the other that led steeply up a mountain, but she suggested I try the pathway perceived as hard. When I stepped upon it, giant boulders dissolved as I placed my foot upon them.

At the summit of this ascent there was a bright being waiting patiently for me. Whenever I had this dream the being was there. I know that it had an early influence on my thinking, for I distinctly remember reflecting on the advice of my guardian angel and championing an impoverished child in kindergarten who was being ridiculed.

The above dream sequence came to me around the time I also saw my faery forms, so I was not very old. One in particular I called the Green Man. He was a life-sized young boy, joyful and impish in demeanour, and was always dressed in forest greens and browns. He would appear and disappear at will, and disappeared forever when I was about five. By his manner and appearance, I knew he was not of this world, but he was still there anyway. I delighted in his company.

Come Boy dance
Oh will you not come?
What wisdom of old
Has struck you dumb?
A slow fire burns in your dark eyes
Telling me that nothing dies.

VI

A Brighter Light

It was on the suggestion of a friend who had a feeling for my material that I attended a weekend seminar for women on spiritual issues sponsored by an Irish organisation. It was taking place in Doolin, County Clare. The group has a base in Dublin, and they are interested in, and responding to, the new energies manifesting themselves worldwide. It was a longer drive from Donegal for my antique car than I had anticipated, which would have deterred me if I had known. I am glad I didn't.

I was immediately made to feel at home by a group of women who were genuine, gentle, and sincere in their manner. The weekend was enhanced by the presence of a psychic healer from the States named Dianne, an elegant blonde who has deeply sensed intuitive feelings for the Irish land and for the nature spirits who reside here with us. It was a comfortable atmosphere for me to talk about my task, and there was actually much more of an affirmation of what I was doing than a curiosity among the attendees. "Well, of course there are faeries, and faery people. And we are not surprised that you are one, for we almost knew that right away. We are glad you have come home."

Moderator Briona was a particularly sensitive and intelligent woman. She helped me understand the power of the changeling myth from a country woman's viewpoint, and how these women helped to sustain these ways of relating truths.

Right away I was introduced to Jaya, who was involved with the same interests as I. It was not hard for me to guess that she was akin to the elfin realm, in one form or another. Her particular talents at the moment are in depicting the little people with visual art, and she had just published a card game similar to a Tarot card layout called the Gaelic Medicine Wheel. The cards are inspired by the mystical tales of the ancient Gaelic people, "and illustrate both the inner and outer states of being, as playfully portrayed by the Irish Gods and Goddesses, the leprechauns and elves, and their mythic and magical animals." (5)

Jaya introduced me to Doreen, who is a "fortune teller" and also frequently uses the Tarot herself. I said I had used tools such as the Tarot as an adjunct in therapy. Sometimes when I was quiet with someone, pictures about their life would simply come into my head, and I would use the Tarot or similar adjunct to give form to the question the person was asking.

Doreen explained gently but firmly that was how the Irish thought. They were naturally intuitive and trusted those ways of knowing, this second sight. She explained that she had a legitimate profession, and was considered a professional, even "with the doctors in Dublin".

I sat there listening to the stories of the women, about the anger of the oppression of Ireland, about how they were asserting themselves as individuals for the first time in history. I listened to the soft and gentle way they related to each other, and to Briona reading poetry in Gaelic.

How was it different from a weekend with Yankee women? While less open than the Americans on some issues, they were also much less intellectual or logical. Far, far less materialistic and goal oriented. On and on the stories came, and they were all from the heart. They were speaking from their intuition, and I realised this was a way of expression that I knew but did not use as they did.

In my country, I had been criticised for not articulating more clearly, or loudly, or precisely. However necessary, it was a way of thinking that was not natural for me.

In the Irish women's group I was being criticised in a gentle supportive way, but criticised nonetheless. This time it was for almost the opposite behaviour; I was too rational, too pedantic, not expressing my feelings in an intuitive way, not relaxing into the moment, not coming from the heart, not using my intuitive pictures to talk, as they did.

This time I also felt uneasy, but beneath the chagrin there was no anger. Rather, shame. A shame that I was hiding behind my academic credentials, and my American upbringing. Hiding that which has actually been the very factor that has taken me anywhere interesting. Hiding my essence. It is the faery in me, if I may put it so simply. They were asking me in their subtle and patient manner to let the faery show. The skill is very ancient in my memory. So embarrassing to let love show, to let joy out, to let laughter become a part of me. Yet, that was my assignment for the weekend.

That evening I walked along the road. The mist rose and mingled with the sky, and there was no noise at all. In the distance were the Aran Islands, where a not too distant relative lived at one time. I thought how lucky I was to be here in this serene part of the world with my sisters who would continue to be patient with me - even though I was an American in need of them.

Soon after the seminar, I went back to a 1992 California Christmas with my family and friends. A gracious time it was, but the faery project still lay very much ahead of me.

In the words of my witty son-in-law, my daughters were reconciling themselves to the emerging reality of having an "itinerant author" as a mother. When I announced my return to Ireland to continue my book on folklore there was mixed reaction.

"Things could be worse," pretty Shelly said, without commenting further about my project. Of my faery granddaughter she hesitantly added, "She lives in an imaginative world of her own. One of my friends said she comes from another planet."

Stars! Infinite alphabet of light
Indecipherable mystery of night:
The writing is too fine
But spells your name...and mine!

"It's too late now for you to go back to your familiar life," gentle Debra added with reflection, "but we all love you."

"We will miss you." bright Lynn said simply. "We don't exactly know what you are doing, but the kids love it. You are a right-on grandmother."

I returned to Donegal in January 1993 with gale force winds blowing at my door, and I again wondered about myself. I didn't take as long a journey as did Pádraic, but I certainly continued to cut further ties to the life I knew.

I now rented The Old Schoolhouse, a stoic establishment which I leased in the preceding fall, since my Gweebarra cottage had been sold. As its name implies, it at one time housed the young children of the area during their school careers. The robust building still retains its stone exterior and high-beamed ceilings. The former master's quarters are now a modern kitchen. There are two bedrooms and a bath, and the spacious feeling of the interior suggests a mountain chalet.

It overlooks majestic Marble Head Bay in the very northern tip of the county, where the secluded sandy beach extends in every direction. The school is only a short distance from where the enigmatic mystic George Russell (pen-name AE), a contemporary of Yeats, used to take his solitary walks at the beginning of this century. He would write of, as well as paint, the "shining ones" he would encounter there while in meditative pose.

It is said that whoever leaves his footprint in the sand of that beach at full moon is destined to return, and one would not be surprised to catch a glimpse of this gigantic man in these surrounds. He would see the *sidhe* (pronounced as "she") - the legendary Irish faery - in visionary form most frequently after being away from a city or town for a time. He sensed that the west coast of Ireland from Donegal to Kerry "seems charged with a magical power", and he found it easier to have his visionary experiences there than elsewhere. No one would disagree.

The great Indian sage Sri Aurobindo spoke of his poetry as "a rare, high and exclusive pinnacle of the soul's greater sight". The sage considered that AE possessed the nearly inexhaustible "well of inspiration" that so typifies the Celtic spirit, temperament and tradition from which the poet drew "a magical and delicate draught of other air. ."

Aurobindo prophesied that "the first waves of the surge of spirit have already broken over the dry beaches of the age of reason", and he felt that AE exemplified this oncoming spiritual force. [6]

A friend of AE's was Sir Arnold Bax, one of England's leading composers and a skilled man of letters. Both men were active in the Dublin literary circles during the days of the Irish renaissance, as were Yeats and James Stephens.

Bax also spent time in western Ireland in his early manhood, and was entranced with the serenity of the area and of the people. He would visit AE on occasion at Marble Hill, where the visionary would go to paint on wet days in a rustic summer cottage in the wooded grounds above the strand. It was loaned to him by his friend Sir Hugh Law, a local political figure and owner of the nearby fine house and estate.

On one occasion, AE was painting at his easel in the middle of the floor of the summer cottage, and Bax was reading quietly in the window seat near the door. Suddenly, something unusual happened. In his autobiography, *Farewell My Youth*, Bax writes of this event:

"I have not met with many experiences which cannot be accounted for by a rational explanation, but one of these occurred in that place in the dripping Breagy woods.

"I suddenly became aware that I was listening to strange sounds, the like of which I had never heard before. They can only be described as a kind of mingling of rippling water and tiny bells tinkled, and yet I could have written them out in ordinary musical notation.

"'Do you hear music?' said AE quietly.

"'I do,' I replied, and even as I spoke utter silence fell. I do not know what it was we both heard that morning and must be content to leave it at that." [7]

Sound of a running river
Embraced by a passing breeze...
I am these

Squirrels, pine-martins
Skittish among the trees...
I am these

Piercing call of the wild duck
When ponds and lakes freeze
I am these

What the hawk longs for
What the barn-owl sees
I am these.

Although beloved by those of mystical persuasion elsewhere, AE's views are not well-known among the rurals. He was considered an outsider of sorts, as were Bax and Law. As a Theosophist, AE's prose would not have been offered in the classroom, nor his poetry read in church.

In mentioning the name of this "daft wanderer", one is not surprised to hear the comment, "He was one who stayed in the big house." The actuality of it is that he often stayed in quite modest circumstances, but his friends were definitely "gentry".[3]

I was given a lead to another faery connection in the Marble Hill area from a seemingly unlikely source one day when two Gardai (policemen) called at the schoolhouse to return my passport and residence card. They'd noticed my harp and asked if I would play for them. So I did. They took a cup of tea and the sergeant, who knew about my research, said:

"Oh, it 'twas Tom McGinley who saw the faeries. He talks about them still. He's a good man to talk to you."

"Aye, he'd be a good one," replied the detective who was with him, nodding in agreement.

It had been on his first visit that the sergeant candidly told of his partner being very wary of the"wee ones".

"Aye, you are studying the faeries. That is good, they are part of our heritage. I had a partner, he's retired now. But there was a place, along that long stretch of bog and lone country south of Gortahork, he wouldn't go anywhere near there. Not even with me. 'That's a faery place,' that's what he said. He'd seen the lights there once, you see, and his family talked about it..."

I followed up the lead that the local Sergeant had given me on McGinley, a farmer living close to Marble Hill. The garda wasn't sure, but had thought McGinley might have been one of the locals who had seen the wee ones at some time.

As it turned out, Tom McGinley did not have too much to say, unusual for an Irishman. "Well, the Sergeant probably thought that living up here in Donegal

that everyone would have a chance to see them. I think he might have me mixed up with somebody else."

A quiet and gentle man, Tom appeared relieved when the spotlight was taken off him and taken up by his articulate wife, Mary. Among other stories, she remembered this about the faeries: "My grandfather said, when he was coming up from Brady Head, from fishing, he was telling everybody what a time he had getting up because they were throwing stones. They were throwin' stones like Billy-O. You know, real fast. He could see nobody, no real person. It was the faeries that were throwing the stones, that's what he thought. Oh, he was a very strong believer in the faeries, you know.

"But in my generation now, I must say, that I never seen one. And I believed very strongly on them until I emigrated away to Belfast in 1945 and then after that my mind broke away from all those things, you can well imagine. That was when I was with my first husband, before he died. Then I came home again."

Her family knew AE as an artist, so presumably he concentrated on his painting career while at Marble Hill. As I was talking to the McGinleys in their modest cottage I spotted an oil painting on the wall. Five faery beings are dancing around an ancient oak tree. Moonlight is shining through the leaves, providing a highlight for the dancers - all costumed in soft, gay colours of blue, yellow, rose. A very unusual adornment for an Irish wall, it was.

"That can't be a George Russell original, can it?" I said, noting the magical style, the lightness of being, the joy.

"Well, you are one intelligent lady, you are. That is who painted that. George Russell rented that house over there for three or four months a year, so my mother would go over and look after him." She pointed to the house across the meadow. It was an unassuming two-story white-washed cottage, but nevertheless had a panoramic view of all of Marble Hill bay.

"So, it was a present for her, and it was handed down to me in my day. We were going to school where you live now, the old schoolhouse, so it wasn't too long ago. It was painted in the woods down there on Marble Hill. You see, that's the moon coming through. Those are faeries, they are. He would see them down there, at night. There was a cottage in the woods he would go to. It was called the faery house, but it is gone now. My mother said he was a nice, quiet man."

After these two leads, I investigated the location of the "faery house". I found that other stories of "music being heard" and similar faery antics have been associated with it. Now disintegrated except for one standing chimney wall, it sat high on a hill overlooking the sea. Silent, quiet, peaceful, a place of uninterrupted tranquillity in the deep woods. Giant rhododendrons bank what once was the cottage yard, and a profusion of wild flowers dance across the forest glens.

I stood on the still remaining ledge of the window seat where Arnold Bax had heard his faery music, and knew I was privileged to be there. Although I heard nothing that day I would not have been surprised if I did.

This is from a story of AE's called *The Avatars*. A central character is talking to his young poet friend, possibly only across the ridge from the cottage:

"It was Midsummer Eve. A faery stillness was in the air. The only glow came from that girdle of green fire which all night long lay about the earth in midsummer nights. Paul and the poet sat on a hillock looking over tide-deserted sand to a long black ridge lying like some monstrous animal half on earth and half crouched in water. There were apparitions like silver stars that glowed and went out and glowed again and ran along the blackness of the ridge.

"'See, the lights of faery!' whispered Paul. 'They hold festival to-night. It is Midsummer Eve. Do you see? Below there on the sands! Those tall flame-coloured people who move in some mystic ritual!'

"'How lovely! How wonderful! Their dance seems to be god-guided. Are they those who never fall out of Eden? They move all with the innocence of unfallen life. Are we to go back to their world?'

"'No...That life lies far behind us. We, I think, shall go back to a brighter light...'" [8]

VII

The Faith

Another contemporary and colleague of AE, American Walter Y. Evans-Wentz, was one who believed in a great deal of what he discovered on his pilgrimage to Ireland at the beginning of this century. He did his undergraduate studies at Stanford University in California and then obtained his doctorate at Oxford University in England. The essence of his doctoral dissertation is contained in his book, *The Fairy-Faith in Celtic Countries*, still in print.

He trudged all over the Celtic lands to obtain first-hand information concerning the presence of the wee people, knocking on cottage doors and being warmly received. He actually did not find anything qualitatively different than I have.

By Celtic fairy faith he meant that specialised form of belief in a spiritual realm inhabited by spiritual beings that has existed from prehistoric times until now in these lands. He felt that the oral tradition of the unlettered country people has maintained elements of the religion of a learned caste, the Druids. The fairy faith in its purest form originated amongst the most highly educated and scientifically minded Celts of ancient times.

Many Irish researchers agree with Wentz's position. Mac Cana tells us that what has been salvaged in printed form is only a fragment of a prolific oral tradition beginning as least as early as the 3rd century B.C., which finds its "closest detailed analogues in the sacred texts of Vedic and classical Sanskrit". [9] Literature written in Irish dates from the second half of the sixth century when monastic scribes utilised the Latin alphabet for that purpose, the native Ogham alphabet being too cumbersome for these extended texts.

The monks worked diligently with the *file*, a poet trained in the oral tradition, who was also the King's companion and counsellor. Both the poet and scholar were preservers of tradition. A successful union it "was the beginning of a working liaison which was to generate the earliest and the richest medieval literature in western Europe. For the next five or six hundred years monastic scholars were to devote themselves to the culturization of the vernacular tradition in a way that cannot be paralleled in other European countries." Although these scholars undoubtedly censored pagan-learned tradition by omission as well as by, in their eyes, correction, they were "saintly pioneers... to be like so many hives into which was gathered the rich scattered honey of oral tradition." [10]

Wentz believed that the natural aspects of Celtic countries impress man and awaken in him some unfamiliar part of himself that gives him an unusual power to know and to feel invisible or psychical influences:

"When there are dark days and stormy nights, let him sit beside a blazing fire of fragrant peat in a peasant's straw-thatched cottage listening to tales of Ireland's golden age - tales of gods, of heroes, of ghosts, and of faeryfolk. If he will do these things, he will know Ireland, and why its people believe in faeries." [11]

He saw the study of the universe in his time as being wholly a study of phenomena and perception, and behind phenomena, there must be the ultimate cause of all things. Science is not limited to that which is only material and visible, but includes a knowing or a knowledge of everything that exists. To consider a materialistic hypothesis as adequate for study of the fairy faith "would not even be reasonable, and, incontestably, would not be scientific".

Wentz was part of the first wave of the turning tide, the "rise of soul against intellect" which both Yeats and AE prophetically proclaimed. "A science of souls seems likely to supersede the prevalent materialist science that recognises only bodies."

His conclusion was that the folk religion of the Celtic peoples cannot be explained away by any known scientific laws. It must presently stand on its own merits. Faeries exist, they are real. "Science" will someday recognise this truth.

We do not count seconds on a clock
But the 'braon ailse '[4] on a rock!

Wentz's intuitive grasp of the "natural aspects" helps us understand why the fairy faith has been so strong, so imaginative and so perpetual in this particular area of the world.

Those who live in the Celtic lands do not need an explanation as to the profound effect this holy land has upon them. They will curse their "pile of rocks", the endless mist on the bog, and the tragic history herein, but their hearts do not leave their homeland, even in exile. They have always been awakened to the knowledge of the great mystery here.

My well educated witty friend Jim from Belfast, who describes himself as a man of no particular authority on the subject, reveals how spontaneous this feeling is:

"I think there is reason to believe the faeries existed. There is too much talk for it not to have some base for it all. Anyone psychic and on the right wave length would be more likely to observe them. The faeries haven't gone, but people just no longer have the ability to see them, or don't allow themselves the ability to see them.

"It has been three generations since my people would have been on the land, but my wife was born on a farm. The generation before my wife believed implicitly in faeries. Those born and reared in the country they were 100% convinced of faeries. In wintertime, the darkness, stormy nights with clouds goin' across. It is quite scary on a country road. There is an awareness of every noise you don't hear in the daytime. It is a silence you don't have in the city."

Distinguished folklorist Katharine Briggs, not a professed believer herself, nevertheless adds that even though the faeries were supposed to have disappeared, "even in the Midlands, now, in the twentieth century, with all its commitment to modern science, people still claim, rather diffidently, that they have encountered the faeries. As for Ireland and the Highlands of Scotland they do not even pretend to think that they have gone, though it is often said that fewer people now believe in them." [12]

I had the privilege of interviewing Cathal Ó Searcaigh, one of Ireland's most noted poets, who composes in his native tongue, Gaelic[5], the language of his people. Cathal understands the mystery from personal experience. His house nestles in a green glen at the foot of Mt. Errigal, high above the Atlantic waters which nearly lap at its base.

The white quartz giant glistens "like the bright confines of another world", and Cathal has lived most of his still-young life in that environment, and knows of these aspects. To the north of Mt. Errigal is Muckish mountain, whose flat plateau would easily accommodate a space ship.

Stand and stare
At the Tail of The White Mare[6]
The Run of The White Cow
Ask why, ask how.
And you will be asking and knitting your brow in a
*   frown*
Until all the stars fall down!

To the west one can see the wild and lovely Tory Island, looking rather like a stone city in the sea. To the south is Benbulben in County Sligo, where Yeats reported the "gentry" have often been seen - those whom AE knew as the "tall, resplendent, shining ones," the *sidhe* who are "not of this world".

Wherever one looks there is quiet beauty, mysterious beauty, ancient beauty. How could one not be a poet here? This from Cathal:

"I think sometimes that what we would call simple people had the ability to see because regimented intellectualisation didn't blockade their sights. They were seeing to a large extent with their third eye. I think that was much stronger in them.

"They had a sense of place, of being rooted, and being close to the elements; the importance of place names, so vitally meaningful to them. People related to the landscape. That hill is called the hill of the Druid fires, that sort of thing. Rooted in tradition, knowing who they were, the importance of the genealogical line in Irish tradition, the ancestral sort of worship, it made it very close to the spirit of these people."

Cathal also commented on the aspect of darkness. It closes in, and brings a stillness with it, almost a meditative mist.

"Darkness was certainly a very tangible reality for those people, for my mother. Darkness. They were brought up in an area like that. Of course, now they would say that electricity has done away with the faeries!

"My mother and my father, they believed always in the otherworld. They professed Christianity and all this, but they were not uncomfortable with that otherworld. They realised with their intuition that it was there, that it was more powerful and more potent than this veneer of 2,000 years.

"When my mother would throw the kitchen water outside at night, she would always pause at the doorway before she did so. It was out of respect for the faeries, so in case they happened to be passing by they would have time to get out of the way. It was a natural, graceful act.

"Christianity in Ireland, although it has been quite successful as a veneer, behind it and beneath it at the same time there remains a solid foundation of pre-Christian religions that were much closer to other dimensions, perhaps more feminine, or matriarchal. We are not the only intelligence, the universe is teeming with life!"

Wentz and AE speak of the golden age inhabited by the "tall resplendent ones - the opalescent beings". Who are these ancient Irish gods? Did they really exist? The speculation varies, but it would be difficult to find an Irish man or woman who would deny their presence altogether.

Dagda, the Good God of Harvest. Breas the Beautiful. Niamh of the Golden Hair. Deirdre of the Sorrows. All of the Tuatha Dé Danann.

We knew them, we knew them all
Some were handsome, some were tall,
We knew them, we knew them well
Those that rose and those that fell.
We followed them as they chased the deer
We drank with them when they made good cheer,
We knew them all along
We shared in their poetry and song:
On sheets of linen, with pillows of lace
We urged the fathering of their race.

The Tuatha are usually considered to have been an actual, historical people, and are called the Irish faery race because not only were they magical in nature, but they were closely associated with the *sidhe* who were their non-human faery colleagues. They all lived a long time ago, before the coming of the Celts. The Tuatha vanquished their predecessors, the Fir Bolgs, not by might but by magic and wit.

Tuatha Dé Danann is translated to mean the "people of the goddess Dana." A feminine goddess she was indeed, the daughter of the god Dagda, the supreme head of the Tuatha. She is associated with ideas of fertility and blessing, and he with ideas of magic and abundance. "He was called the Dagdae, for it was he who performed miracles and saw to the weather and the harvest, and that is why he was called the Good God."

Much scholarly investigation and speculation have been done on the origin of the Tuatha Dé Danann of Ireland. One version is that the belief in them gradually developed from belief in primitive spirits of vegetation, and that they were the mythical gods of the Celts. Another view has suggested that the Tuatha were historical beings, their original home being Greece. Still another source thought that they were most likely immigrating Phoenicians, as this would account for their sophisticated powers.

More poetically, the transmigrate Tuan MacCarell of early Celtic literary legend said they came to Ireland "out of heaven" and since he was known to be King of the Deer in Ireland at one time, many Irish prefer this rendition of their origin. "Who could doubt such a King?" - they reason.

After the official introduction of Christianity in AD 431, records became somewhat accurately kept:

"When the Tuatha-De-Danann had remained seven years in the north of Scotland, they passed over to Ireland and landed in the north of this country on a May Monday. They then burned their ships. After this, the Tuatha-De-Danann, surrounded themselves with a magical mist for three days, so that none of the Fir-Bolgs could perceive them until they had reached Sliabh-an-Iarainn..." [13]

Later tradition embroidered this into a narrative telling how they had sojourned in the mysterious northern islands prior to this arrival, bringing with them "incomparable esoteric knowledge" and four gifts from the four great cities found there, Falias, Gorias, Finias, and Murias, places which "certainly have no place in terrestrial geography".

From Falias came the Stone of Destiny, and it confirmed the election of a rightful monarch by roaring under him as he took his place on it. "The stone would give such a shouting noise that it was hard from sea to sea, throughout the whole Kingdom, which presently would satisfie the party standing on the stone, and all the Rest of his future fortune to the Right of the Crowen..." [14] The High-Kings of Ireland were so crowned.

The invincible sword of Lugh was the gift from Gorias, and no one could escape from it when it was drawn from its scabbard. From Finias came the magic spear of Nuada, no victory could be won against it; and from Murias, the cauldron of the Dagda. This vessel had the property of being able to feed as many as required without ever being emptied, and "no company would go away unsatisfied".

The gifts have been associated with the four elements by esoteric observers. The Stone has been linked with the element earth; the Spear with fire; the Sword with air; and the Cauldron with water.

The Tuatha "came to invade Ireland, against the Firbolgs; and they gave battle to each other. The Firbolgs were vanquished and slaughtered in the battle." [15] They spread "druidically formed showers and fog-sustaining shower-clouds over the country, and caused the air to pour down fire and blood upon the Fir Bolgs." [16]

Moreover, the hand of Nuadhat, the beloved King of the Tuatha, was cut off in this same battle. Since he was rendered imperfect by the loss of his hand, by law he was obliged to abdicate the kingship and was succeeded by Breas. The rule of Breas brought only hardship for the Tuatha.

Diancecht and Credne, both magicians, "put a silver hand upon" Nuadhat which had been "welded withe a piece of refined silver...They formed the hand in motion in every finger and joint, and...Mich, the son of Diancecht, to excel his father, took off this hand, and infused feeling and motion into every joint and vein of it, as if it were a natural hand..." [17] He was known thereafter as Nuadhat of the Silver Hand, and he resumed his Kingship.

"The people, Tuathy De Danaan, ruled Ireland for 197 years; that they were most notable magicians, and would work wonderful thinges by magick ... wherein they were exceedingly well skilled, and in these days accompted the chiefest in the world in that profession." [18] "Thereby; when they pleased, they would troble Both sea and Land, darken Both sonn and Moone at theire pleasures." [19]

This family of Dana are represented in the ancient texts as epitomising all that is good and beautiful. They were "the fairest of form, the most distinguished in their equipment and apparel and their skill in music and playing, the most gifted in mind and temperament that ever came to Ireland." [20] Endowed with divine power to combat the forces of evil, their enemies embodied the forces of darkness. Being of divine origin, the Tuatha remain the Race of Light.

A description of Etain contained in Leahy's *Heroic Romances* illustrates the beauty of the prose. Leahy's translation was from a 15th century manuscript, but the actual story is found in much more ancient sources, the date which tradition assigns to events related in the tale is about B.C. 100. Etain was not only the fairest maiden in all of Ireland and consort of the High King, but from the faery haunts herself:

"A clear comb of silver was held in her hand, the comb was adorned with gold; and near her, as for washing, was a basin of silver whereon four birds had been chased, and there were little bright gems of carbuncles on the rims of the basin. A bright purple mantle waved round her; and beneath it was another mantle ornamented with silver fringes: the outer mantle was clasped over her bosom with a golden brooch.

A tunic she wore with a long hood that might cover her head attached to it; it was stiff and glossy with green silk beneath red embroidery of gold, and was clasped over her breasts with marvellously wrought clasps of silver and gold; so that men saw the bright gold and the green silk flashing against the sun. On her head were two tresses of golden hair, and each tress had been plaited into four strands; at the end of each strand was a little ball of gold. And there was that maiden undoing her hair that she might wash it, her two arms out through the armholes of her smock.

Each of her two arms was as white as the snow of a single night, and each of her cheeks was as rosy as the foxglove. Even and small were the teeth in her head, and they shone like pearls. Her eyes were as blue as a hyacinth, her lips delicate and crimson; very high, soft and white were her shoulders.

Tender, polished and white were her wrists; her fingers long and of great whiteness; her nails were beautiful and pink. White as snow, or the foam of a wave, was her neck; long was it, slender, and as soft as silk. Smooth and white were her thighs; her knees were round and firm and white; her ankles were as straight as the rule of a carpenter.

Her feet were slim and as white as the ocean's foam; evenly set were her eyes; her eyebrows were of a bluish black, such as you see upon the shell of a beetle. Never a maid fairer than she, or more worthy of love, was till then seen by the eyes of men; and it seemed to them that she must be one of those that have come from the faery mounds..." [21]

The world in which the Tuatha reigned supremely eventually ended with the arrival of the Sons of Mil, the Milesians. After the faery people's defeat in battle, Amergin, poet and judge of the newcomers, is said to have divided Ireland in two.

The half of Ireland that was underground he gave to Tuatha Dé Danann, and the other half to the Sons of Mil. The Tuatha then "went into hills and faery regions, so that faeries underground were subject to them... Henceforth, the Tuatha occupy those hidden and external regions, the mound-dwellings and the islands." [22]

The Danann were defeated by the Milesians but they did not withdraw: "By their magic art they cast over themselves a veil of invisibility, which they can put on or off as they choose. There are two Irelands henceforward, the spiritual and the earthly. The Danaans dwell in the spiritual Ireland, which is portioned out among them by their great overlord, the Dagda.

"Where the human eye can see but green mounds and ramparts, the relics of ruined fortresses or sepulchres, there rise the faery palaces of the defeated divinities; there they hold their revels in eternal sunshine, nourished by the magic meat and ale that give them undying youth and beauty; and thence they come forth at times to mingle with mortal men in love or in war... To this day the Land of Youth and its inhabitants live in the imagination of the Irish peasant." [23]

This belief was traditional at least as early as the seventh century as evidenced by a clerical biographer of St. Patrick who refers to the "sidh or gods who dwell in the earth".

They come and go from their underground chambers at will, or sometimes reside in the mountain tops or the clouds themselves. This is really quite a common speculation, and it is taken seriously, not poetically. The Irish invariably are aware of their legends and hold strong opinions. To them, the Tuatha live in their memory, not their imagination. One of the country men I interviewed by name of Nolan responded characteristically:

"The Tuatha were a race that lived here before the Celts came, and the Fir Bolgs before them. They were defeated by the invading Celts and retreated into the hills. Their descendants are the faeries."

VIII

Who Coaxes the Lichen?

The ancient traditions were kept alive orally by the often-time unlettered, but not uneducated, country people. The belief in the magical persisted through the centuries-old art of the storyteller, the seanchaí (pronounced shankey), who through his form of art handed down this treasure generation after generation.

A seanchaí is a sort of medium in a very real sense, and existed as an integral community leader. Until quite recently each rural area had its own story-teller, generally an old man, sometimes a clever woman, who combined a rich store of folklore with the ability to tell a story well. Neighbours and travellers would gather nightly at the fireside to listen to the tales, to talk over the news, the famine, the faery.

Wentz emphasised this, and my Donegal landlady's father, Paddy, spoke likewise from his boyhood memories:

"Can you imagine what this small cabin would have been like by candlelight, or even gas light? The quietness, the darkness outside. The rain and the wind, and he telling' the stories by this kind of light. The light would flicker around the room, on that wall there. And such a voice he had. Oh, it was magic. It was magic. We all listened, we were all part of it you see."

The storyteller's genius was respected and there was an understanding of the importance of the position. The storyteller passed on his or her magic in a highly personal way, in candlelight by an open turf fire, through expression of voice and gesture. It was a true art form, one which simply could not have been kept alive in the dryness of books.

The history of collecting this orally transmitted folklore in Ireland goes back at least as far as the beginning of the 19th century, when both scholars and promoters alike recognised its value. With the government's creation of the Irish Folklore Commission in the early 1930's, the tales were then primarily collected by men of the countryside.

Off they went, eager young men, with their bulky Ediphone recording equipment strapped to their bicycles to collect this priceless heritage. Their versatile vehicles served the dual purpose of transportation and electrical source. Upon arrival at their destination, they would bring the bike into the house, and upend it, as if repairing a flat. A small generator was attached to the bicycle which was then connected to the recording equipment, and as they turned the pedal on the bike, it gave a power supply to the recorders.

Since 1971 the Commission has been incorporated within the Department of Irish Folklore of University College, Dublin. By 1979 there were nearly 2,000 volumes of manuscripts in the library. A national treasure.

This collection of previously unpublished literature of Ireland is not merely parochial, it is emphasised, but is of international importance. Light is thrown on the history of the whole of Western European people, as this orally preserved literature of Ireland once characterised a much vaster area. The archives in the Folklore Department rank among the richest in the world. Varied and humourous, they are studied by scholars from all parts of the globe.

In addition to the regular manuscripts, in the 1930's and 40's, the help of thousands of National School children was enlisted to record as many as possible of the stories still remembered by the old people of their locality. This enlightened move resulted in a collection of the children's hand-written records which are all held intact by the Department, many in local libraries. They were instructed to collect stories about their areas, and produced delightful ones concerning themselves with memories their elders had about local cures, riddles, forges, food, the famine, weather lore, and fairy-lore. How many are about the faeries and their antics? Of the ones written in English, I estimate about one out of ten. Tales of the faeries, the little ones, the leprechauns, the faery woman, the faery man.

We are with the bee in her flight
And we sing it over and over and over:
Follow follow follow the light -
Flowers await and the blooming clover.

In 1991, an exhibition was mounted at the College showing many of these records together with original drawings. Many of the original contributors, now in their seventies, travelled from all over Ireland to see them.

One who works in this tradition - a man of impeccable reputation - is Seán Ó hEochaidh, currently living in retirement in Gortahork. White-haired and robustly featured, he looks as if he might have been chiselled from the granite rocks of his native Donegal. Scholarly achievements attest to his versatility: as well as being a man of the people, his dedication as a gatherer of folklore earned him an honourary doctorate from the National University of Ireland.

Seán was hired as the Irish Folklore Commission's first collector when he was a fisherman, sailing out of his native port of Teelin. For at least 48 years, this dedicated man trudged the hills, islands, and villages of Donegal to obtain his stories.

He interviewed over 1,500 seanchaithe who preserved the oral tradition of the countryside by recital in evening candlelight. Many times he was the last man to sit attentively at their turf fires and listen to their tales before the advent of "civilisation". Seán's book, *Fairy Legends from Donegal*, was published in 1956 by the Commission.

Seán was kind enough to grant me several interviews, even though in the beginning he had only a vague idea of who I was or what I wanted. He has been used to a particular form of notoriety, especially among the Folklore students from all over the world. Seán said:

"I have been asked time and again about the faery faith in Donegal. I invariably give the reply that the faery faith is as much alive today, especially with the older folk, as it had been a thousand years ago. In many Gaeltacht areas the seanchaí's art and imagination resisted the technological erosion of the twentieth century up until quite recently, at least.

"These people, I'm very much afraid, are fighting a losing battle at the moment but they have handed down to us in oral tradition a link in a chain which brings us back through the mists of time and indeed to say the least of it, they have left us with a very rich inheritance..."

Seán himself hedged on whether he believes in the faeries he has studied for decades, but he is hardly unaware of the mysteries of rural Ireland. As often happens, an informant will start out with the statement, "I don't believe in them myself, but..." Then they will tell a story that affirms the fairy-faith much more than it denies it. The following memory of Seán's is an example of that response:

"It happened in 1954, on 16 December 1954, to be exact. I had an aunt married in a townland called Rhanakille close to Teelin. My Uncle and I used to visit her regularly. He was her brother, you see. We went there maybe a couple of nights a week. Ah, before these nights that I am telling you about, the fishermen were all out and there was very good herring fishing. But the weather changed, and they couldn't get out anymore.

"We were at the aunt's house and we went down to the pier because we were drying a net that my uncle had spread out. It was a lovely moonlight night. Lovely. Full moon. We were coming back about 10 o'clock. Shortly after we went down to the boat, we left and came up to our own house, which was on the roadside too. This man was walkin' up the road in front of us. I said to my Uncle, 'Doesn't that man walk like Mickey?' That would be his uncle, and my grand-uncle.

"We walked fast, and no matter how fast we walked we couldn't get up to him. When we came up towards our house, he turned in and he went in. Me grandfather was in the house readin' the paper, and he heard the latch being pulled, but nobody came in.

"When we went in, we looked around you see. We thought Mickey should have been there, but he wasn't there at all. So we asked, 'Did anybody come in?'

"'No,' he said, 'a few minutes ago somebody pulled the latch there, but nobody came in.'

"So that was all right, we forgot all about it. The following day, Mickey went to the bog for a creel of turf, and on the way back Mickey fell dead at one o'clock that same day. Now, I checked with his daughters who were in the house with him if he was out anywhere on the previous night, and he wasn't out of the house.

"Now that was a funny sort of experience that I had. I could swear that it was Mickey from his gait, his shape, and his size, and the way he walked. But he wasn't out of the house that night! Wasn't that peculiar?"

Not any more peculiar than the faery sightings in these environs. These gentle beings, what did they look like when seen? Seán gives us an educated description.

"What sort of beings (tribe) were these faeries? The old people had many names for them. The generic name for them was *sidheoga* (she-oh-gee) but they were more generally called wee folk; good people, gentry, *bunadh na gcnoc*, the people of the hills, the merry host, etc., etc.

"They were without a doubt a small people. They have often been described to me by "seeing celebrities" as people of not more than three feet tall; well built in proportion, red-haired, and usually wearing bright coloured clothing. They wore pointed shoes whenever they wore them at all adorned with white buckles. They had the reputation of being great cobblers."

Who coaxes the lichen?
Who whispers to moss?
When trees grieve their foliage
Who comforts their loss?
Who is it talks to the chattering brook?
Who cautions the bat in his hideaway nook
Of frost and no more flies?
We who tell no lies!

When Seán talks of the "seeing celebrities" he is speaking of those who have reported on having had direct faery contacts. These people who "see" often acquire a celebrity status of sorts locally, hence the term. His following story is a typical description of a surprise encounter. Seán insisted it was true, "My grandfather believed it really happened anyway":

"Me grandfather, he told us a story. He not only told us, he told it to the Parish Priest as well. When he was young and a growin' up lad, there was an old woman in the neighbourhood. Instead of goin' to church on Sunday, they sometimes went into this old woman's house and they prayed with her. Church was so far away, you see.

"Then when they got their prayers over they went out. There was a wee bit of a meadow just above her house. They played an old fashioned game of hurley. For that hurley, they used just an ordinary hazel stick, called in Gaelic - *Camán*, with a turn in the top like your walking stick. Instead of what they use now, they skinned a rabbit and dried the skin. Then they filled it full of hay or soft leaves and sewed it up. That was the ball that they had.

"So, they were playin' and me grandfather broke his stick. There was sort of a shrubbery just above where they were playing the football, and he saw a branch he could use as a stick. He broke it, but the skin was so tough on it, he had to twist it, and twist it, and twist it. And when he give a half a dozen twists, and what comes up right out of the root of the stick but a man! A wee man!

"He gave a full description of the clothes that he wore. He was a broad shouldered man wearing a blue coat and green pants. His vest was red, and he wore the peaked cap of a sailor. So, naturally grandfather was frightened and he ran like blazes. When he was only about 200 or 300 yards away and on his doorstep, he dropped the stick. It was two or three months before he went outside the house again."

A particularly willing "seeing celebrity" I was to meet in this place of power was a man named Joseph, although he would certainly be quite surprised to hear himself described as a celebrity. Joseph is a strongly built, grey-haired countryman in his middle years, an earth-mover by profession. He has the body and stance to go with that job. A no-nonsense man's man, he has lived in northern Donegal on a remote part of the Fanad peninsula all his life. Fanad is isolated in itself, and the old ways have remained to a refreshing extent.

Who or what are we?
Sap in a tree!
Why are we here?
To peer -
Dance
Prance
Float, glide
Kiss a bride!
Who?
Peek-a-boo!
Why?
To laugh and cry!

Since the little people have been his "good neighbours" for as long back as he can remember, it does not appear that he is worried about being thought odd because he sees faeries. His grandfather talked of frequent encounters, as did others in his Fanad peninsula, especially in his grandfather's generation and before. He is more self-assured and less defensive about what he has experienced than many are, whose "otherworld" encounters do not correspond with what their particular cultural rules say about such matters. His understated way of speaking makes him quite believable.

When I first interviewed him, Joseph appraised me with a firm look. He was quite able to take on whatever challenge the stranger lady would bring him. It was apparent to me that there were two analysts in the room.

After a bit he decided I was safe to talk to, and he did not stop talking after that. Affable and extroverted, he gave the same amount of energy to the faeries as his next favourite topic of interest which was the acquisition by the Irish government of the island of Rockall. This is actually no more than a rock in the ocean north-west of Ireland but its ownership would extend fishing and other rights from the mainland to the adjacent waters, especially relevant to the hardy fishermen of Donegal.

After we became acquainted Joseph offered to take me to the top of Knockalla mountain to where he had his own personal contact with the faeries, and I gladly accepted. It was a perfect summer Sunday in Donegal, and his side of the mountain overlooks the sandy strand of Portsalon, described as one of the most beautiful beaches in the world. As we journeyed, he described his experiences:

"Well, two or three donkeys and I would head up this way here. Two creels of turf on each donkey, home and dump your load and go back again. A lot of people would do the same job. These donkeys, they would be snuffin' (trying to mount) each other, and there could be a donkey upended, with a big load on him.

"Way back when I was about twelve, I used to come up this path here, and more men would come up that path yonder, and still more up from that road. Come that direction, and all would head up that track there, and cross over across the hill and up the mountain to Glenvar Chapel every Sunday morning. Summer and winter. Aye, women too, about two dozen of us. Me and the boys goin' to Mass and creelin' the peats. Here, by this stream, we'd have a drink of nice fresh water. Meself and my father, we would come up here to hunt hare and grouse and woodcock, and beyond that hill there is a lake with wild ducks and swans.

"We used to go creelin' peat, now up this mountain. The faeries. This old fellow he used to tell me about this rock called the 'faery cradle'. I'll show you now. There are two places there. The first place I saw them, see that side of the hill there, see that rock. Aye. I'd seen them there, that's the faery cradle. Then this stone down here, this flat stone, low to the ground. Now it is covered over now. This is all grown up, like. That's called the faery cradle too.

"The first time I saw the faeries was at that rock. I was frightened then, afraid in the beginnin'. I was maybe eight, nine at the time. Well, I didn't know what to make of it. I told my grandfather what I saw and he said to me, 'You needn't be afraid of them. They won't touch you. That's just the faeries.'

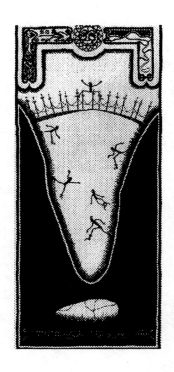

"Oh, he saw them too, Aye. There'd be another old man who saw them too, but he is dead now as well...The old boys were tellin' me they weren't after me, and not to be scared of them.

"There were a group of these faeries up walkin' around. They seemed to be dancing. I was about fifty or sixty yards from them. Other times I was as close as 15 or 20 feet. They were roughly about two feet tall, all the same size. They appeared to me like ordinary people, only they were small. Apart from that, I can see no difference, except they were wee. I never seen any little ones, any children.

"Two dozen and three dozen, a lot of people. Men and women. Aye. On the rock and around the rock, and they were dressed like ordinary people. They had red caps on, and like red coats, they were mostly in red. They had slightly different colours of hair. I couldn't say I saw any that had red hair. They'd be fairhaired or black, brownish.

"Some of them were sittin', and some of them were dancin', and they seemed to be playin' some sort of musical instrument. Cause I could hear it. They'd make noise but I couldn't make out what they were saying.

We talk to each
  in their own tongue
And sing each song
  as it should be sung -
We talk to stones
  To mouldering bones,
The grey seal
  The slippery eel
And their sons and daughters
  Inhabiting waters
And cry
  To the eagle in the sky

"I'd see them for maybe five, ten minutes. They seemed to be relaxed, it's hard to explain it, like. But they would take notice now when they saw me there. Oh, they looked at me. Aye, they'd know I was there.

"They'd carry on and then they seemed to just fade. You'd be lookin' at them and they'd just fade away, like a ghost. They'd be there for ten or fifteen minutes before they'd fade. You'd be surprised then!

"I don't know how many times I seen them since. Oh, my God, I saw them dozens and dozens of times. Sometimes a group, sometimes less. I didn't always see them in the same place. I would see them in different places, but that was the first place. I went there maybe two years afterwards and I saw nobody, but then there were times I would go there and I would see one. So, it makes you wonder...

"I used to go out to some of these trees out in the fields and people used to tell me they were faery trees, but I went to places like that and I never saw nothing. But then you'd go to a place where you'd expect to see nothin' and then all of a sudden you'd see them.

"Now, a lot of people are tellin' me I imagine what I see. But you don't imagine it, there's no way. They can appear and disappear very fast, like. That's what I think, anyway.

"That house with the thatched roof on it, the man who lived there used to tell a lot of stories about the faeries. And my grandfather, he believed as well. But then you'd tell other people, and they'd be laughing at you. They wouldn't believe them. But then there were so many people that did see them, you know.

"I'd like to see them again now. Aye," he said wistfully. "I'd be lookin' forward. I'd like to see them today."

It was a good four-hour hike up the side of the mountain and back down again to his childhood home. Joseph appeared to be enjoying his role as tour director, not only showing me where the faeries are seen but the location of a once-operating still for the local variety of poteen. We came across three or four small stone circles not far from the faery cradle, and what appeared to be the remnants of some ancient adjacent structure. An enchanted place, it was.

He looked across the field and told me the following story, told sincerely but with some hesitation:

"Now, I hadn't had a drink for a month, so you couldn't put it down to the drink. And I hadn't been takin' any tablets. No, nothing. But I happened to look across and I saw this thing comin' straight down. Aye, in daylight. Just like that, look. Slowly down. I couldn't believe me two eyes.

"I told my wife Sally, and I told some of the girls. It reminded me of a big house or a big round building. Lit down like that. I never heard anyone else talkin' about it. That was about two years ago. Nobody seemed to have seen it. Nobody saw nothin'. So, to this day, I am baffled as to what it could have been. I am certain that I saw something. I watched it for maybe two minutes comin' straight down, like a helicopter. There seemed to be windows, and I could see it so clear, away in the distance.

"I don't know how you'd explain it. It was down there by the football field. That's where I estimated it was. Next time I was over there, I thought maybe a plane had crashed there. When it passed down, I was waitin' to hear some noise. Like a plane crash you'd hear. No, but there was nothin'. Silence. A massive machine of some kind."

As we came down the hill, his nieces and nephews greeted us with enthusiasm. "Did you see any faeries today, did you see any?"

"No, we did not," Joseph replied. Yet we all knew they were there.

Another gentle man, John, who lives not far south of Joseph on the outskirts of a small town called Convoy, recounted his story to me. He is the proud owner of a museum of farm equipment and vehicles, all lovingly put into better shape than they were originally by his artful expertise. His immaculately furnished parlour shelved some of the trophies he had won in local agricultural shows for his efforts at this restoration.

John had an encounter with a "wee faery woman". It was long, long ago that he met her, nearly a half-century ago. He grew to manhood, married and had a successful business, but he never forgot the faery woman. He told me the story, and then showed me the very spot where he saw her, although he wouldn't go down to the woods himself.

The wooded area is less than an acre, and a stream runs through it. The fields have been ploughed right up to the edge of it, but it has remained untouched. How it was determined how much land to leave alone was not clear, but the property wasn't even owned by John's family. "Nobody has ploughed there, you see, since I saw the wee woman." His story, exactly as recounted to me:

"I only saw them once, and I was only thirteen years of age at the time when I saw it. Well, there is a wee plantation (wooded area) up the road, where there is a lot of shrubbery and trees around. At that time the turf would be damp and I was set to gathering some kindling. I'd been there before many times, just gettin'

the wee sticks, you know. So I was down this evenin' after school and had about half my work done, and I looks down and I sees this wee woman, all dressed in tartan, cap and all. All in red, she was.

"She all of a sudden appeared. All of a sudden. It appeared to me she just come out of nowhere. She was standin' there, and I looked at her. I broke a few more sticks, and I thought she was comin' at me - that she took a notion to me - so I wasn't long goin' away. I thought maybe she was after me. You know what a wee boy of thirteen would think.

"In her face she looked like an ordinary person, just. Except that she was only about 2 feet tall. There was no way she was a person, no way. She wasn't a small woman, no way. No woman looked like that. And in the particular place she was in, there would be no small women, you know what I mean? It was a desolate place where there would be nobody. Not at all, not at all. Our house was the nearest to it, and then right around was all the plantation.

"It wasn't long until I was at home, I can tell you that. She didn't disappear, I disappeared! She was still there. To tell you the truth, I didn't look too much at her. When I saw she was comin' nearer I didn't want to be there. Nowadays, I would stand and look more at her... maybe not!

"Many was the time I had been down in that wee place where I saw the faery before that time, and I saw nothin'. I must have been further in, then, that time. In their territory, you see. I never went back there from that day to this day."

John and Joseph maintain an active correspondence. They have started what I would call a support-group since they recently met each other through a local talk show in Letterkenny, County Donegal - the subject matter being that of true faery sightings.

This local interest was brought to light by a fellow American writer, Scott S. Smith, who also believes in the presence of the little ones. Not long ago he sent notices to Irish newspapers that he was conducting a serious study on the faery folk and wanted to hear from anyone claiming to have had such an experience.

Most of the replies he received were from the Donegal area, and there was such a strong interest in the subject the radio station invited him to be a participant. Joseph has invited me to be a member of this support group, although he wouldn't describe it as such.

One farmer from the Mourne mountains reported seeing red-vested creatures dancing in the fields one stormy night. When asked if it might have been children instead that he saw playing there, his quick reply was, "No child would be out in this weather."

Playwright J.M. Synge, while spending time on the Aran islands, was given much information about the faeries from the Aranites, many of whom were staunch believers. One of his acquaintances, Pat Dirane, had seen a good many of them, especially in the sandy districts next to the slip. They were described as about a yard high, with caps pulled down over their faces. On an occasion Pat saw them playing ball just above the slip, and warned Synge to avoid the place after nightfall as they might do him mischief.

A most typical current story about the faeries is like this one collected from Paddy and Nora, the parents of my Irish landlady, sweet Mary of Gweebarra. I was always treated royally when I called on them, but on my first visit Paddy nearly outdid himself with what I would call "canned blarney", thinking this would please me, the Yank.

Memorised stories, witty fantasy. Perceptive and intelligent, he soon realised I didn't want anything spectacular, not even anything clever. I just wanted their personal opinions on the matter, that was what was important. It was then they spoke with authority and from the heart.

"Well, it was a very common thing here to believe in the faeries in days gone by. They were very gentle, but it didn't do to interfere with them. Some say you'd get rich sometimes, that they'd give you money. And they always wore a red cloak. And they were very gentle. Aye. Old people believed terrible in faeries. They wouldn't like to do anything that wasn't right in case that they would hurt them.

"The faeries were a colony of their own, all right. They were a gentle race, you see, that lived by themselves - they had no contact at all with any other body. No, no. But, the ghosts and the dead people, they were the ones who died way back. They would be local people, you see.

"You know that moss that grows in the Glen? They said that the faeries pulled it up and dried it in the summer time and that was their bed. They took it up in the mountains where they lived. That was their bed for the night.

"And the mulberries, there is plenty of them up there in the mountains for them to eat. They were natural. They'd eat the berries. Aye, they were our natural neighbours."

Vincent, a Donegal fiddler, spoke in a similar fashion:

"We called them the hill-folk, we did. They lived up in the woods, Quinn's Woods, it was called. They were seen up until 1940. They said they used to hang their wash out...but I don't know. They were like badgers, you see...up there in the woods. You left them alone like the other wildlife."

We are where the woodbine grows
And the wild rose

Dew on the thorn,
In its shimmer we are born.

Now and tomorrow
Until the end of sorrow...

IX

The Faeries Question

There is quite a bit of conjecture among the country folk on what has happened to these natural neighbours since they are no longer seen around as much as they once were. As we have seen, they are sometimes thought of as being descendants or relatives of the Tuatha Dé Danann, in which case we need not be too concerned as to their eventual fate.

Yet, the faeries are not always associated with the Tuatha. Sometimes they are thought to be fallen angels, definitely undesirable aliens. There is almost universal belief among the Irish that the faeries are not an integral, or at least a desirable, part of the "father's kingdom". Apologies are made for them, and tenderness and protective feelings are felt for them, but that is often the extent of the charity felt for these social outcasts.

This problem of origin and thus of eventual outcome of the faeries is sometimes referred to as "The Faeries Question" and is known all over Ireland. It is often taken literally by the country people, who often can become emotionally involved in the faeries' dilemma. The question is: "Will the faery host go to heaven?"

A many-versioned story encourages us to believe that there is still hope for these "fallen" faeries.

A priest met a party of the Good People who had come to ask him their ultimate question. He rebuked them and answered, "You will never enter heaven until this dry dead stick which I have in my hand bears leaves, flowers, and fruit." He threw the stick on the ground and left them crying and lamenting, but the next day the dry stick was found bearing not only leaves but flowers and fruit as well.

Delia of Connemara emphasises the usual explanation as to why they are no longer so numerous. They have been banished by the power of the Church:

"The faeries be gone now. They used to see them, that's a fact. The Priests said a Mass every day and they put them at rest. Those people are at rest because you don't hear or see them anymore."

A more detailed explanation is given by Michael, the retired garda in Roundstone, and neighbour of Delia. As he mused about the past, he decided that the faeries simply left in the same manner as did so many of Ireland's youth:

"Oh, yes, the Céilé. That was very common, you know, in those days in the west of Ireland, but all over Ireland, really. The belief was all over Ireland. Ireland was an Irish speaking country part of this century and before that. There are only small pockets left now.

"There wasn't any other form of entertainment except to visit each other's house. They'd have poteen. Then, when they got a few glasses of that, they'd loosen their tongues, then they'd sing and talk and tell stories and they would entertain each other. A very simple way. They'd talk of the faery then, they would. But no more. They have been forgotten...the leprechaun, he emigrated a long time ago."

Since the Irish are very inventive, there are other versions. "At Ballynahinch we were told that they were blown away by a great storm."

"They went to Scotland."

An expression that is heard many times is, "It was better for the land before they went away."

Or, "They have gone - gone like the wild geese."

An impromptu response was given me by a gentleman who lives on the western tip of the Dingle peninsula. In no time at all he established himself as an authority, pretty much on any subject of query. He told me that the faeries used to be about, "but they left the area with the coming of the Black and Tan in 1916. Into the graveyards they went, into the graveyards. Underneath the tombstones they are hiding. Into the graveyards, up there, they still are."

This was done to escape from the slaughter by the English cavalry, he explained. "They are still in the graveyards, afraid to come out because of what the Black and Tan did. That's why the faeries have disappeared."

Although he had a twinkle in his eye, this story was told as if he were a guide at one of the sacred sites. He believed it.

The fear of faery is consistently expressed, regardless of these population statistics. A young woman in Connemara, showing a fairly typical scramble of ideas and demonstrating considerable anxiety about the subject said:

"We grew up with a fear of the faeries, whereas now there is no time to think about faeries. We have other fears - there is more fear now of the living than of the dead. Well, there would be people who would be more aware of the spirits than other people. They say you are better to believe than not. To know about them and disbelieve is more dangerous than not believing."

A very fearful Connemara man, James, now in his eighties, shows how clearly the faeries are mixed up with spirits of the dead. As he talked, every few sentences he would say, "I never saw any myself, thank God." The remark in itself seemed to serve as a safety measure.

"Oh, I don't know. It is very hard to understand. They were plentiful years ago, but they are not plentiful now, because when you are out travelin' in the world there is the cars and the motorbike, and they have lights and everything. But long ago when they used to be walkin' and goin' far away walkin' and goin' to some other places, then you'd see them...

"When we go sittin' in the houses they'd be all talkin' about them. They'd be talkin' about the faeries. I never saw any myself, thank God. We used to be goin' through houses that were empty. People would be gone from them. We'd be goin' along the shores, long distances, and we never saw any of them. That's it, we never did. Thank God.

"I remember this fellow, he was visitin' and he was goin' to a dance, and then he was goin' home. He got afraid in the house where the dance was, and so he called his neighbour out when he was leavin'.

"So the neighbour came out, and he had to go about 200 yards or more to be with him. But when he was walkin' through this field he heard some moanin', and the wife came out, and this man was standing there before them like that on the ground.

"Now, he was dead and gone. He was drowned in America. He was McDerman, and McDerman was talkin' to this fellow. He told him to tell his mother or father that he got a bottle of poteen somewhere, but he didn't pay for the poteen, and to tell his parents to pay for the poteen.

"And that he'd be all right. Now, that's the truth. It is really hard to manage them, you know. It is very easy for you to get afraid like, when you meet a person like that."

He was clearly expressing anxiety when he talked of this, recalling the times he was out late at night and would fret about such an encounter. Although he mixes up the faeries and ghosts, it was also clear from his descriptions that they were also thought of as separate. A faery is one thing, a ghost another; but a faery can apparently masquerade as many other things, including the living and the dead:

"Another time my father and the Priest...they were comin' to a village there, and there was a bend in the road. They were halfway there, and this woman was standing at the side of the road. She was well-dressed, you know, and she put up her hand. But the Father, he didn't stop. He carried on. 'Only for us to be in the car tonight,' he said. 'Otherwise you'd have one of them as passenger.' The Priests, they was afraid of the faeries, too."

He went on to explain that there weren't any women in Connemara then wearing that kind of clothes, and they wouldn't be out at night anyway. So, it was immediately suspected that she was a faery woman in disguise - one of "them".

A well-dressed lady wandering around those hills at night was rarer than a week without rain.

The following leprechaun has a relatively stable appearance as he has apparently been seen in a similar fashion by more than one person. The locale of this sighting is just outside of the town of Gortahork, County Donegal, on a path that winds down to the sea. I have walked there, but was not fortunate enough to meet the little man.

The comment to follow about being an Ulster Protestant is well understood in Ireland, but not necessarily elsewhere. It is a common belief among the locals, especially the Catholics, that the austere nature of Ulster Protestantism has ruled out the belief in anything so nonsensical as a faery. My Belfast friend Jim gave me this story and explained, "The Catholics banned the faeries, but the Protestants forbid the thought of them!

"I do know someone who swears she saw one in Donegal - herself and her husband - they were both down-to-earth Ulster Protestants. She was a teacher, and they were holidaying in northern Donegal, and this day they saw a path goin' down to the beach, and they took it. She saw a very small man about two feet tall, with a hat on him and a cutaway coat. He was sittin' in a stone ditch, smokin' a pipe. She stopped and said to her husband, 'Did you see it?'

"Now, her husband, who was not as down-to-earth as she was, said, 'I did, but I wasn't going to let you know I saw it.'

"The small man looked up, jumped over the ditch to the far side. The couple were a wee bit afraid, but walked to where he had been sitting and there was no trace of him. No trace of him. The land is fairly barren in those parts, so he couldn't have hidden anywhere. This was around 1980. She still claims it happened, just like I said."

A storyteller and historian from the town of Clonegal by name of Willie claims this to be "impeccably true" as he knows the participants well:

"The story goes, this particular man, John O'Brien was bulldozing a ditch in the middle of two fields. He was taking the ditch out, you see. This particular stone, a fairly big boulder, came to the blade of the machine and he gave it a good few heaves, as usual, to move it to be level with the rest of the field. It did give a bit of a lurch, and as soon as it gave the lurch he was amazed to see a little figure with a green coat 2 $\frac{1}{2}$ feet high jump out from behind the stone.

"The little one scurried down the ditch as fast as his little legs could carry him. The men - there was another man with him - the two men were both petrified. They stood looking at the little one, and he got into this little grove of trees.

"Now, they did stop what they were doing and go down and look in the trees but, needless to say, saw nothing. But they swear that it was 11 o'clock in the morning, they weren't drunk, they hadn't double-vision, and they firmly believed and nothing would convince them otherwise, that they saw one of the little people!"

Another one of these elfin beings, called The Thornhill Faery, was reputedly seen by at least a half dozen people over a span of nearly a century in an ancient family location. It was described thus to author McManus by an apparently reliable informant:

"Small though he was, he was perfectly proportioned, and he wore what were the traditional clothes of the country a century or more before. He had a green, brimless, "flowerpot" hat; a closefitting, green, cutaway tail coat; a yellowish waistcoat and a cravat; buff knee breeches, and grey woollen stockings, and on his feet were brogues. His clothes were clean and neat and in good condition. He was cleanshaven, his eyes were blue, and his hair light brown." [24]

Why do I hide
and from whom?
From time's busy loom!

Where am I found?
Where there is no sound

Save the curlew's evening cry
Streaking across a painted sky.

The shape-changing capacity of the faeries has not gone unnoticed. Spirit has told us that there is an essential individuality to a given faery, but they are quite capable of putting on a different costume each day. So they appear naturally unpredictable and surprising. A country man expressed the matter very well to collector Lady Gregory:

"As to what they look like, they'll change colour and shape and clothes while you look round. Bracket caps they always wear. There is a king and a queen and a fool in each house of them, that is true enough - but they would do you no harm. The king and the queen are kind and gentle, and whatever you'll ask them for they'll give it. You might speak to them if you'd meet them on the road, and they'd answer you, if you'd speak civil and quiet and show respect, and not be laughing or humbugging - they wouldn't like that." [25]

In case anyone thinks faeries no longer exist in the twentieth century, author Campbell told of the following events which took place relatively recently in Donegal. This group of faery pranksters seem to be very adept at shape-changing.

In 1976 a car full of teenagers was coming home from a dance in Glencolumbkille, along the Meenaveen road "when they saw in the distance an unusual light, and little folk making merry. As they drew nearer to the sight they stopped their car and listened to the music - which resembled the sounds of Irish music. Suddenly they became quite frightened, and were glad as their car sped away from this place, and its mysterious inhabitants. They told their stories to their families but no one believed them." [26]

Some months later a local man was in the same spot cutting turf, and suddenly saw a little man coming along the ridge of the bank riding on what appeared to be a fox. The little man told him to gather up his tools and go home as quickly as his legs would carry him. He ran, jumped on his bike, and made off for the closest town, where he reported his experiences to the Garda. What the Garda in rural Ireland may do about such an situation is highly speculative. As the sergeant from my area pointed out, there are as many believers in the little people among these civil servants as anyone else. They would not make jest of it, nor necessarily assume that it was because "he had the drink in him". Too many times they have heard or seen strange things themselves. It is unlikely that they would investigate such a sighting alone, and never during a full moon.

We are many
and we are one
Dancing rays
of the glittering sun
Drops from the same cloudy vault
From golden grain a single malt
Join with us and take a sup
From the one cup!

X

Nation of Their Own

According to the country people, the faeries are a nation of their own, concerned with their own needs and rights. This is particularly true with regards to property issues.

The raths in Ireland, sometimes known as moats or Danish forts, are pointed out as the abode of the faery communities. They are circular hillocks and are found all over, especially where the land lends itself to this type of mounding. Disturbing their habitation by any means of altering these areas is considered unlucky and believed to entail discomfort if not disaster on the transgressor and his kin unless restitution is made. All over Ireland this idea was conveyed to me consistently. "People wouldn't touch a bush or any of those things under any

circumstances, if it is connected to a rath. Absolutely. My parents were adamant about that."

As stated earlier, one reason usually given for these raths being faery property is that they were originally the sites of the homes of the legendary faery people of Ireland, the Tuatha Dé Danann. Sometimes they were supposed to have buried their dead in these barrows.

"Oh, they still talk about the faeries. And they still got those raths, those things where the faeries were. They won't touch those things, they never cut the trees down. They are sacred, you see. They don't want to interfere with the faeries house, you know."

This is a recent story about a rath in County Meath. If this same farmer had been born a couple of generations ago, he undoubtedly would not have ploughed down the rath, as community opinion would have been decidedly against it:

"This farmer, he had a rath. He was sowing wheat and barley on it. He ploughed the rath down because he wanted more crops. It had been there forever, the rath. Twice he sowed it and twice he tried to reap it. Each time he sowed the grain came up, it formed a complete round circle just where the rath had been. And the grain never rose beyond a few inches, much less than the height of the regular grain.

"After the second year, he left it because when he tried to reap it the binder broke, the thresher on the combine. It's a true story. The binder broke the second time he tried to reap it. And it formed a perfect circle, a perfect circle. He never interfered after that with the rath."

Swirl and eddy
Rise and fall
Flux is at the heart of it all

That bad luck ensued after disturbing any faery property is demonstrated by this story. Variations of this theme are still told regularly all over Ireland. This story comes from the School Children's collection, housed in the Letterkenny, County Donegal, library. The locale is only an hour away from the Old Schoolhouse, my residence. Anyone who wants to can go to the libraries and read these stories:

"When a gang of workmen were engaged in constructing a new road in the townland of Mounthall, they encountered a hawthorn bush directly in their path. The foreman in charge gave orders to some of the men to have it removed. Several of them in turn declined to perform the task, declaring that the bush was a faery-tree and that they would be inviting disaster if they interfered in any way with it.

"One of their number however, by name Jim Gallen, declared that their fears were only rubbish and that he would prove it by removing the tree himself. He went for a hedge-knife and began.

"He first began to remove the small boulders round the foot of the tree and was rather startled, but not discouraged, when several white mice emerged. He next proceeded to extract the bush roots and all. When he succeeded in uprooting it a large bird of queer shape and without any feathers flew out in his face and then disappeared.

"Then the worst fears of the men came true. Jim Gallen's cows suddenly refused to give any milk. This was very strange for they did not seem to be ailing. Things went to such a pitch that in despair Gallen went and planted the tree again near where he had uprooted it. He was very much relieved the next morning to find that his cows were overflowing with milk." [27]

My experience would also indicate that there are indeed some queer birds in Donegal. Once I was walking in the forest, vaguely hoping to meet up with some faeries. It was a moody day, but an educated glance to the west indicated that the rain was busy elsewhere for awhile.

I looked up to the sky as a comical looking black bird had caught the corner of my eye. It looked somewhat like a wind-up toy, or a kite, but it was much too far up to be either one. If you thought a bird could be Raggedy Ann, that is what you would call this one. Then, it simply disappeared. Misperception, thought I. Something in my eye. About a half hour later, it flew back overhead again, this time across a then cloudless expanse. Higher up, it repeated its disappearing act. There was nowhere for it to go, but it was gone. This created the need for me to stare at other "real" birds, to see if somehow they just looked like they vanished in some way. No.

As I had taken the long loop around the trail, it took me another hour to return. The black bird did not return, and the whole of it slipped my mind. Suddenly, on the crest of the hill the bird appeared for the third time, sailing above the trees. Then, it simply cut out, as if it slipped sideways through a wall. As if the sky were a shell it could penetrate. There was no way out, but it went out anyway.

It was around this time that John, of the agricultural museum, showed me a faery thorn on his property, not too far from where he sighted the faery woman. It was just as he described, an unsightly clump right in the middle of a ploughed field. The story goes:

"My nephew was tellin' me some time ago - they have in a field what we locally call a rowan - a wee clump of bushes, you know - and it was all hangin' out past him and was always in his way, and so they took down the hook and they allowed him to cut this one down. They had cut one down, and the next one he cut down, a stem fell and went in his head there. That finished him cuttin'. Aye, it is a funny place up there.

"There was a gentleman who was a farmer. He had a rowan, and he cut it down, and there were stones in it and he took them away. He went in the next morning to his byre, where he had the cows, and there were two of them lying dead. So it was supposed to be because he disturbed the gentry. That's what we call the faeries up here. The gentry."

A similar account is told by my friend Jim from Belfast:

"The principal offence was in interfering with an isolated thorn tree, or a rath. The thorn tree looked so utterly ridiculous - sometimes four fields would be combined into one and the harvesters in these big fields would have to go around one isolated thorn tree. You couldn't even break off a twig.

"My brother in law, Johnnie, removed a branch which had rotted from a thorn tree. He took it away and he dumped it, and his mother was quite annoyed at him for touching it at all. He was only 28, and he laughed at her superstitious beliefs.

"The next morning, his best animal, a cow, stepped on a rusty can and had to be put down. His mother said, 'I told you something would happen if you touched that faery tree.'

"He never touched it again, I will tell you! He brought the rotted branch back the next day, thereafter no one ever touched it.

"Children could play around and in the thorn tree and break branches without repercussion. You had to be an adult with the intent in order to suffer the faery wrath."

Jim continued with the following story. It is particularly valuable because not only is it quite recent, but he insists that it happened in just the way he has related it:

"An immense factory was being built on this site in County Antrim. They were building it, within the last 20 years. They were clearing the site, and they had modern equipment. One thorn tree still remained on the property. The local boys cleared everything else, but none of the machine operators who were local would chop it down or interfere with it in any way. The company finally got an Englishman to remove it. He chopped the tree down and then bulldozed the roots.

"The next stage was putting in the piles, concrete pilings which were approximately 12 inches in diameter and 10 feet long - to give a foundation.

"They laid the first of the foundation with a pile driver, but when they returned the next morning, the pilings were 3 feet from where they should have been! Their location had been moved!

"The construction bosses thought that somehow a mistake had been made. So, they got a new length of piles and again placed them into the ground. The next morning, the pilings were again 3 feet from their original location, but in the opposite direction of the first move!

"So they called a conference to see who was guilty. The first group of engineers swore their measurements were accurate, and the second team also so swore that their measurements were true. There was confusion. The smallest man in the meeting, he stood up and said, 'The only way you are going to build your factory here is to replace our tree where it was.'

"So they said to him, 'How can we, it has been cut.'

"He said, 'Get it grafted.'

"Nobody believed him initially of course. As they were discussing alternatives, he left the room, as he said he had to go to the restroom. Nobody knew him, no one had seen him before, and after he had gone, he was not seen again.

"They mentioned the small man to the local foreman and he said, 'That's a faery. What did he tell you to do?'

"They told him, and the foreman said, 'If you have any sense, you will do just that.'

"So they brought a tree specialist from Holland in. He replanted the roots on the tree and grafted it. There is now a wee courtyard in the middle of the factory, with the thorn tree growing. The faery man was never seen again, but the thorn tree thrives.

"A top man told me that. It is printed in their journal, although they would probably deny it now."

He told the story to me as if there was nothing particularly improbable about the vanishing faery man. It was the movement of the posts that was of interest to him. "Well, you know. He just disappeared...like they do."

Interfering with the faery paths can lead to some unusual consequences. Houses with unstable conditions of one sort of another were reported to me all over Ireland. In one estate the grass would grow back overnight after being cut. In another case, the chairs in a certain room would change positions during the night, although this poltergeist phenomenon was attributed to a deceased former owner rather than faery mischief. This report concerns itself with erratic locks and was told to me by a sincere, industrious farmer who lives in the hills of County Carlow. He fully believed every word, and it did not appear that he questioned how it happened. He went on to tell me the names of the people who lived there, and where they moved to after they left the house with the open-door policy.

"Well, there is a house about four miles from here, at King's Cross. Well, it is still there. The door on that house couldn't be locked at night. If you locked the door when you'd be goin' to bed it would be opened in the mornin'. The house was built on a faery path, and it never could be locked.

"There was people who only stopped in it for a couple of years, and then someone else took it over and the same thing happened to them. The door couldn't be locked! No doors could be locked. None of them would be left shut, they'd all open themselves. The windows be undisturbed, but the doors would be open."

The consensus is that one is going to have troubles if one builds directly on a faery path. Many anecdotes tell of concerns about trespassing on faery property. Often a wise woman is consulted. One such woman, after inspecting a house that was suspect, declared that a corner of it must be removed as it was interfering with the progress of the "good people". The owners did not hesitate to take her advice, and the problems ceased. Another one didn't follow the advice of the local expert on faery paths, and continued to be plagued with bad luck.

When building a house, one precaution was to erect four posts on a proposed building site for a house, and if the posts remained in position this was a sign that the "faery host" approved. Another method was to put a spade into the ground. If it remained upright, the faery green light was given.

Disorientation is another common result of encountering purported faery displeasure. It is often called being "led astray" and a typical description often involves a time-space mixup, although recovery always occurs. In this contribution, the country man Nolan is talking about the "gap". This is simply a gap in a hedge. This experience happened to him long ago, maybe 30 years, and he remembers it vividly. The emotional tone is still there in the telling of the tale. He was coming home from a dance across his very own field of his youth.

"Oh, I knew the path well, now. The path led to the beach. It was about 11 o'clock at night. I knew the fields and the path as well as I know my hand, and I was comin' back to this valley and into this field. There was no way I could get through, and I was lookin' for the gap to come through, but there was no way I could find the gap! There were hedges and trees, and the hedges, they looked 100 feet high to me, that's how they looked.

"And I sat down in the ditch, and I was sittin' in the ditch for about an hour and all of a sudden the whole thing brightened up, and I knew where I was. They say somebody leads you astray."

This one is from the library collection:

"I know a fort in Taylor's Field. This one is called 'Taylor's Fort'. It is round in shape. There is a fence of bushes round it. If any thing goes near it, or if the man ploughs over the fort something is going to happen to him.

"There is another fort above it called the King's Grave because one of the Danish Kings was running away from the Irish and was killed and was buried there. This fort is square. If any person works on it he is sure to wander. One day a man ploughed over it, and he wandered. His two horses died in the morning and the plough was broken so that it could never be fixed again.

"This second fort has no fence around it. It is covered with grass and the field has always to be kept ploughed, because if it were not you would not know it from the other grass. In that way you might step on it and wander.

As above
So below
This we know
From long ago.

"Faeries are supposed to live in them. Music was often heard in the fort in Taylor's Field." [28]

The faerywinds are frequently mentioned, and what this means is anybody's guess. It is particularly reported on during the equinoxes.

This is from Ó Duilearga's collection:

"Ever since I got any sense I have been hearing the old people say that when the wind whirls the Faery Host is in it, and the name they had for this wind was the whirlwind (*sidhe-gaoithe*).

"This haystack (was securely fastened) and the wind came very suddenly and powerfully and hit the haycock, and lifted it up into the sky. The props were knocked east and west. The wrackrope was lifted from the front, itself and its stone, and thrown as far back as the rope stretched. Nothing would convince the old people that it was not the Faery Host that was in the wind." [29]

Delia of Connemara was quite serious and adamant on her recall of these events:

"There was this one Sunday there and my father was lookin' out the door. Well, it was the first of May, and they say the faeries do change, the faeries, the faeries. They say it is dangerous to be on the streets the first of May.

"Oh, my father came in and told us about it. We went out and we seen all them. Millions of them, oh yes. They were showing, and then I stacks the hay, and then they got a new home, whatever they want. They change where they are livin'. They want to change to a new place, now. All the leaves, like the leaves of the tree. Then they got up, and then they hit a wall. They were tiny things, you know. Then they went over the sea, and the walls, and the hay, big stacks of hay and all. Then we didn't see them no more."

Moving stones, another mysterious event, are also frequently associated with the faeries' activities. These stones, with the strange power of returning home, are found in most parts of Ireland.

I like this story as it has my great-grandfather's name associated with it. Grandma Sprague's father was a Gorman from County Meath: her mother was from the Scots Huntley clan. A hybrid marriage of two cultures. "This of course caused great difficulties," my mother would say to me as a child. My father would then add, "You see, it is the Irish problem. It goes back for centuries." This would sum it up for them, but not for me. What could go back for centuries to a child? Perhaps I am just beginning to understand now, living here and knowing this land a little. All my relatives would believe this story, though:

"It seems a fisherman took a stone from the ruined wall of Gorman Church near Malin Head, County Donegal. He put the stone into his boat intending to use it as a floating anchor, but when he put it overboard, it seemed to get loose from the rope that was attached to it and, apparently, sank. When he got home, he found that the stone was back in its place in the church wall. Needless to say, he left it there!"

Another story about a stone with the power of locomotion was related to me by my mystical friend Ted from the Dingle peninsula: "This is a true story. They would be in-laws of mine. This happened on the outskirts of Tralee, where they had a farm. There was a field on their property that had long ago been named the Field of the Golden Pig. They were ploughing this field anyway, these two old boys, and it came onto dinnertime.

"Just before dinner they removed a stone. They didn't dig it up. They were ploughing the ground, and they went a bit deep and the ploughshare probably got stuck on the stone. It was a large, square stone. It was so unusual, the stone, that they thought there might be something under it, something sacred.

"But anyway, they went to lift it and just as they were lifting it, they got terribly hungry. An immense hunger came over them. They said they were going to their dinner, right then. So they went to their dinner, and they came out again. When they came out they couldn't find any trace of the stone. It was completely gone, like it was never there.

"The old boys could never locate the stone afterwards. It just wasn't there at all. They thought the faeries took it, because maybe there was something beneath it they were guarding.

"It was called the Field of the Golden Pig, and I reckon there was probably something buried there - a sacred druid idol. Because the druids, long ago, worshipped various objects and animals."

This narrative about rambling rocks was told to me by three separate people in the village of Clonegal early on:

"What happened was, they were clearing this field, and they moved some stones that were on a rath so they could do some planting and plough around it easier. Big stones, they were. It took three men and the machine to move them, and

94

they put them over at the end of the field. Big stones, they were. You couldn't move them without equipment. Then the very next day they were found right back where they started from. Right back on the rath! Nobody moved them back, they moved by themselves in the middle of the night.

"This buddy of mine, he talked to the man who owned the land after he had heard that he moved the stones.

"'I thought you were moving the stones,' he said.

"'No,' said the man.

"'You are having me on,' my buddy said.

"'We did move them,' the farmer said, and his face was shining with embarrassment as he said that!

"This only happened a couple of years ago, when he was working here. The stones, you see, they went back to the rath. That's where they belonged, I guess."

XI

The Chords of Feeling

That the faeries are associated with music and are inordinately addicted to dancing all observers agree. Such associations usually seem to be beneficial in character, although serious time-space dislocation often also occurs with these encounters. People can be "taken away", but the choice seems to be theirs. Stories are told about pipers or fiddlers who disappeared into a cave a long time ago and whose music may still be heard. Michael of Connemara told me this:

"It was also alleged that pipers and musicians - fiddlers and violinists, mostly pipers would be going along the road at night. Tramping the road, maybe. They'd sit down, maybe, beside a rath. You wouldn't know that it was a rath or a lis. He'd fall asleep, and the next thing is he'd find himself inside, brought in by the faeries to play for them. He'd play away, and when he disappeared he was thought to be probably dead. They'd treat him well, and keep him there playing, give him food and drink. And when they disappeared, years may have passed, but to him it was just like overnight."

There are many accounts of the music played by the faeries themselves. Some of the most beautiful of the antique Irish folk melodies are traditionally supposed to have been overheard by mortal harpers or pipers at the revels of the Faery Folk. Folklorist Lady Wilde, mother of Oscar Wilde, said they are as wild and capricious as the faery nature. These delicate harmonies, "with their mystic, mournful rhythms, seem to touch the deepest chords of feelings, or to fill the sunshine with laughter, according to the mood of the players."

Uí Ógáin, in researching over thirty recent legends about music learned from the faeries, finds that usually faery music is heard and faery dancing is seen by people late at night "as midnight and moonlight are used constantly in the

accounts and increase the mysterious, unearthly aspect of the music. The instruments played by the faeries are usually the pipes or the fiddle...the pipes can produce an unearthly sound, evocative of the otherworld..."

The encounter usually takes place at a locality associated with the otherworld, a rath, a meadow, bridge, near the hills or near the woods "and so the scene is set for the encounter between mortal and otherworld and the transmission of music".

In most cases the musician hears faery music and memorises it so he can play it again, and Uí Ógáin reports that there usually is no particular reason given for these events, "except that the quality of the music is so unusually beautiful and sweet that the mortal musician is drawn to it and learns it..."

Usually the gift from the faeries is of benefit to the receiver, but in some versions of the legends because of the respect and fear which faeries were generally held people who played became ill, or even dying as a result. [30]

The harp is mentioned:

"One day a gentleman entered a cabin in the County Clare, and saw a young girl about twenty seated by the fire, chanting a melancholy song, without settled words or music. On inquiry he was told she had once heard their faery harp, and those who hear it lose all memory of love or hate, forget all things, and never more have any other sound in their ears save the soft music of the faery harp, and when the spell is broken, they die." [31]

When I was about eight years old, I developed a passion for the harp. A neighbouring family, the Karlstroms, had many sons, and we children were often in and out of each others' houses in random fashion, like popcorn popping. Yet, I would often tarry in their living room because in it resided a harp, the most beautiful object I had ever seen. When Mrs. Karlstrom played upon it, I was spellbound - the loveliest sound I had ever heard.

Even though it wasn't family tradition, my parents honoured my fascination. I acquired a harp of my own, and this patient lady was my first teacher. Had my life taken a different direction, I might have made the harp my career. As things stood, it was to become an avocation, a form of meditation.

Only recently I found that my favourite composers were considered by Theosophical writer Scott to be "Deva inspired". Cesar Franck admitted that he could hear the tones of the Angels of the Mass and used to try to reproduce these "voices" in his music. Grieg in his *Peer Gynt Suite* captured the elemental life of Norway - "he has caught the very sounds of the earth-elementals".

What could be more faery-like than Tchaikovsky's *Waltz of the Flowers* with its harp cadenza - a glorious introduction? And, according to Scott, "Debussy was the first composer to turn entirely from the human and write Nature-music pure and simple." [32]

Just as close to my heart is the music I now play on my harp, traditional airs written for the Irish harp - many boldly claimed to have been inspired by the faeries; and the music of the Irish harpist Turlough Carolan, who died in 1738 and left behind him over 200 tunes. One is titled *Sidh Beag Agus Sidh Mór*[8], translated *Little and Large Faeries*. It is light and humourous music, but sophisticated. From the Manx contributions come many tunes with faery connections, including *The Song of the Water Kelpie*, the *Fairies' Reel*, and *The Washing Song*. [33]

Legends surround many of these tunes. The man who collected *The Washing Song* used to walk down by a farm stream in the early morning and hear "Themselves" singing the song as they washed their babies. This is concerned with the Kelpie:

"In the long ago, a curiously shaped boat would be seen at the close of a summer evening coming from Bradda towards Dalby. In the boat sat an old man with long white hair, who rowed until off the point. There he rested his oars and sang this melody, which runs up and down the minor scale with the lilt of the waves. As the thing became known, people would come and stay on the shore to listen to his music, for it was very sweet to them; but his boat was far off and no words could be distinguished. When the old man had made an end to the song, he rowed westward till he was seen no more. And no one knew whence he came or whither he went, nor who he was; but the people of Dalby knew his song and taught it to their children's children." [34]

A particularly poetic example of the music of the eighteenth-century itinerant harpers is from Edward Bunting's collection. This romantic and poignant verse is quite faery in feeling. In Irish it reads:

MÁIRE ÓG NA gCIABH
Young Marie of the Tresses

A Mháire óg na gciabb, cuir do dhóchas i nDia,
Ná h-ísligh is ná h-árdaigh is ná fágaibh mé i bpian,
Nó rachad thar sliabh, mar chomhnuigheas an fiadh,
Imeasc na ngleanntán ag déanamh leanndubh gur leat do chaill mé mo
* chiall.*

Siúbhlafaidh mé an tslighe agus na bóithre so síos,
Mar bhfuil an stáid-bhean chiúin mhodhmhar, 'sí thoigfeadh an
* tuirse so dhíom.*
Le glór binn a cinn bhéarfadh an rón glas ón dtuinn,
An crón-torc ón gceo-chnoc is an smóilín ón gcoill.

TRANSLATION

Young Marie of the tresses, put your trust in God,
Do not lower, do not raise, and do not leave me in pain,
Or I shall go over the mountain, where the deer abides, Amid
 the glens,
Grieving because you have cost me my senses.

I shall walk the pathway and down these roads,
Where lives the quiet, modest fair girl who will lift this
 weariness from me.
At the sweet sound of her voice the grey seal will come from
 the waves,
The brown boar from the misty hill, and the little thrush from the wood.
(35)

Vincent, the fiddler from Donegal, would not have a problem in picking up the tune. He is a musician of considerable repute in the Glenties area of the county, his skill being completely self-taught like so many fine musicians in the rural areas. In the aural tradition, he listened, and became a master. Although Vincent considers himself an old-timer because he associates with the old ways, he is actually perhaps only in his late fifties - a tall, handsome man. Vincent explained the power the faeries have to inspire:

"The faeries had their own power, they did. And you see, religion didn't want their power, but their power was still there. I suppose that is the way it is with religion...so it was a matter of power. The faeries were a part of nature, with the dancin' and all that. Enchanted, enchanted, they were. Of the old time. I believe meself there was such a thing as the faeries. I really believe their music, you know.

"You know how someone who wants to learn of a musician. He becomes enchanted of the musician, and then he can be just like him. He can imitate him, like. It was like that when people got their power from the faeries. They became enchanted and then they had the power of the faeries."

Sing sing
Let laughter ring!

In dingle and dale
In every vale
Let laughter tingle!

Every girl and every boy -
Fruit of your joy -

Sing sing-a-ling!
Let laughter ring

And ripple and soar on high
Till teardrops glisten in your eye!

For Vincent, this form of inspiration was very real, it was very much part of his personal life, it was the way in which the muse touched him. When he was describing the above scene, it was as if he was recalling being in the presence of a beloved teacher. He wanted to assure me that he did not copy the faeries, and so his use of the word "imitate" was not what he really meant. Rather, they implanted or infused their "power" through him. It was a joint effort, and he was also creating along with them. He became their medium of expression, but in a very integrated sense. Grateful for his musical talents, he was equally proud of his teachers. He describes:

"First they called them céilí, but around these parts they called them rakin'. You would rake from house to house, and sometimes they would call it rambling. I have a tune I play meself, it is called '*The Glen Man's Ramble*'.

"And the house dancin' was on until daylight in the mornin', and the custom was just beginnin' to die out when I was young, around 1940-1945. It was really strong in my mother's time. Everyone made their own clothes, and that's the way that it was done...the spinning wheels would come and they would card the wool for two full days, and they would do all the wool for her and spin the yarn, and that evening there would be a céilí, all would get-together...to pass the whole of winter tellin' stories, dancin'...it was all handed down, you see.

"Life was different. It was quieter, and you had plenty of time to learn things. Plenty of time to think...there was a lot lost of this way of life, but a lot was recorded in the music...the young people are beginning to play the tunes again, in their own way, the ones that were kept.

"A pastime before things changed was tellin' faery stories. The stories were told that the faeries used to come to different people to their weddings to play. They played one time...They had a wedding and they started dancin' and this piper came in and he started playin'. And they never heard the like of him before, but he played all night and he played the same tune, but they danced all the different dances to this one tune! And it was told by this woman that the father and the mother next door came to the wedding, and they got all their own children to bed, and told the oldest boy to mind the house until they came back in the morning.

"So, when the whole thing got silent and they went to the dance, the lad slipped out of his house and went by the back door where the party was. So he listened there and then he went home again. There were a lot of musicians at that wedding but none of them picked up the tune of the wee piper. And so the folks there, they decided the wee piper was a faery man. Oh, you would know he was a faery man. They throw magic, you see, so you can't remember.

"So in the morning everyone got up, and the young fellow who was listening at the back door, he started whistlin' the tune of the wee piper. His father asked him how he knew that tune, and it was then they all knew he was listenin' at the back door. He was the only one who could remember the tune. He wasn't in the spell, you see. And he grew up to be recognised as a good musician. "

Quite often it is reported that the music in these visitations directly inspires a change of career. This is an illustration:

"It is said that a young lad of the MacCrimmons wished to become a great piper but though he tried hard it was clear even to himself that he lacked inspiration.

"As he sat on a faery hill, a beautiful lady appeared before him and asked him why he was so sad. When he told her, she handed him a silver chanter and told him to play it. As he played he realised that nobody had ever played such music and with its help he became the greatest piper in Scotland and the founder of a famous musical family." [36]

Although we were considerably less than a famed musical family, when we would go to my Auntie Ruth's house at night, there would be singing around the piano. She was the only one in my father's family able to successfully carry a tune and remember words, but it didn't stop the rest from participating. How sweet those times were.

I was always in awe of Auntie Ruth. Even though Auntie was often widowed she managed to acquire one husband after another, never even granting so much as a serious kiss until the knot was tied. All of them died sequentially of quite respectable medical problems, leaving her richer after each arrangement.

Her last nuptial venture took place when she was ninety. Uncle Jack called one day and said he had some "startling" news about his sister Ruth. Naturally, we thought that Auntie Ruth had finally decided to emigrate to her next life. After all, she was elderly and had already raised a fine family and buried three spouses with dignity.

But, she was not through yet. Uncle Jack's news was that she had remarried. A further astounding announcement was that she and her new husband had moved to a retirement home in Montana, to an area that is quite similar in climate to Siberia. I loved her for doing that. Yet alas, her fourth husband died at the age of ninety-five. By last family letter, she is still alive.

This story about the faery music and raths was given to me by Nolan of County Carlow, the one who was led astray. He happily took me on a tour of the site, the Ring of the Rath. High on a hill in the middle of the County, it is a well-preserved circular stone enclosure surrounded by another larger, deteriorating stone circle overgrown with brush. Though impressive even by Irish standards, it is still nothing an agile boy couldn't climb over. One would not expect to see a musical group congregate at such a location, even a faery one. At the time of my visit a husky white horse named Charlie was in charge of guarding the place, doing a rather haphazard job at his task. Nolan's account:

"There is queer things that happened around there, on the rath. There used to be music playin' there every night, around half past two. In that rath, that centre rath. I know several people who went up to listen to it. Now, they said no one could be seen, but they HEARD it. Music was heard up there. A brother of mine said he heard it. A couple of nights he passed by there, he said he could hear it. He said he often stopped to listen to it playin'. It was like accordion playin'. They used to be at it years ago. It wasn't so long ago, 30 years ago or so."

Like Nolan's brother, many people have heard the faery music or antics, without actually seeing them. Ellen was another. She and her husband live close to the base of bold Muckish mountain in Donegal, and to get to their cottage one needs to travel on a very narrow, very windy road. Even though Ellen wanted to hide her enthusiasm with a rationality she thought an American like myself might appreciate, her Celtic way of thinking still fortunately showed through:

"This came to my mind. My mom and dad - God rest my dad - used to visit my grandmother every Sunday night. To do this they went near a bog and there was an old garden there, way back hundreds of years. The remains of a ditch was all around the garden, and my mom and dad always went down that way. This particular Sunday my mom wasn't able to go, so my father went alone. He came home and he told my mother that he heard the faeries marching. He heard them marching.

"Now, my father was like myself. He would not be persuaded of anything frivolous. But my father heard the faeries marching, he said. Never until the day he died did my father ever go near that garden again. It was like marching, like soldiers marching, that is what he said. It had to be the faeries, he said, it couldn't be anyone else. It wasn't in the times of the troubles, or anything like that.

"But my dad didn't believe in the faeries, like myself. I never believed in these things. I liked listenin' to the stories, but I wouldn't say that I was one that would be lookin' for the faeries, you know. But I did hear the *sidhe*, that's the Irish faery, and it was the most beautiful music.

"My husband and I were coming home from a dance. You know, the dances in those days you'd get in at six o'clock in the morning. We came along a long stretch of tall grasses in this bog. I used to love it there when I was a child because it was very mysterious, and there was a lot of places you could sit down and play house and that. I used to herd cows quite near to it, but this night my husband and I were comin' across the bog. We came the near way because it was such a lovely night, it took about a mile off the main journey. We just come across through the tall grass and I heard this music. Oh, it was the music of the *sidhe*, it was beautiful music.

"I can still hear it, but I don't think I could describe it. Oh, it was their music because it had these sorts of lovely notes to it, it had a roundabout - you could feel the atmosphere round about it. There was a mild wind that came with it, and then this lovely music. It had a tune to it.

"I asked dad, 'Did you hear that?'

"He said, 'No.'

"'But surely you must have heard it,' I said.

"Surely he could have heard the music. But it was a long time ago. I never heard anything since of that nature, but I heard stories about it."

Music of old, of another time
-No reason, no rhyme-
Here, here, come here, come here,
Music from another sphere

Music of the world's heaving pain
In seasonal refrain

Music of light and darkness too
The rosy dawn that turns to blue

Music that is water falling
Now the 'conairt sí'⁹ are calling -

Music of old, of another time
- No reason, no rhyme -
Here, here, come here, come here,
Music from another sphere.

XII

The Vanishing Folk

A nother phenomenon reported repeatedly is that of the "disappearing faery people". They are almost always called faery people rather than just disappearers. They are often distinguished from apparitions of the deceased, who also play these tricks, but apparently not as often as the faeries.

What is generally reported is that someone is seen walking down a road, sitting on a bench, or walking across a bog, in a manner that may or may not be suspect. Then, without warning, the person and their gear suddenly disappear, seemingly without any particular provocation. The person is not someone they have known, so it is "not one of the departed. God rest them."

When I first heard of this, I thought the informant was sincere but perhaps had simply made some explainable error of perception. However, I have heard of so many such incidents since then that my current opinion is that they do, from our perspective, simply vanish, like the Raggedy Ann birds in Donegal. Here is one recollection:

"This man who talked about the faeries a lot was tellin' me this story one time. They were eatin' supper in their house, and it was a very cold, wet night. They heard a knockin' at the door, and there was a wee woman about 2 feet high. This wee woman come in, and they asked her if she would eat anything, and she said she would. They were havin' poundies (potato cakes) for their supper so she ate some of the poundies. Then somebody asked her if she had far to go, and she said, 'Not very far.'

"They couldn't get over the size of her, she was so little. But this man told me that he saw a faery before, you know. But anyway, the wee woman left and some of the boys went after her to see where she went. But she went up and she just disappeared in the rock! In just a flash she was gone! That old man he just died last year, but I have him on the tape player."

The following story illustrates how imbedded in the psyche the idea of other-dimensional realities is with the local people. Until quite recently, in many localities in Ireland, it was assumed that everyone who walked a country lane would be known or recognised, especially at night. Nor would they pass without extending a greeting of some sort. My friend Michael tells the story:

"It was about 1950 - around that time, anyway. We were over at a lake, and it was an unfamiliar area. We were on the way back and we were walking the road. Me pal and me. And we were passing an old school that was on our way.

"Just as we were passing the school we saw a man - a tall man with his back to the school door. As we were approaching, the person walked across in front of us. I could hear the grating of the sand under his hobnailed boots. Now I was a stranger in this area, and I didn't know whether the person was dead or alive. It could have been anybody as far as that's concerned. I happened to be a stranger.

"So, he walked maybe 10 yards in front of me, across the road to the other side, and we didn't see him anymore. He just disappeared, he just vanished, you know.

"Now, a thing that is strange about that person - whether he was dead or alive, or a faery or a *sidhe* - was that he didn't speak to us at all! And so once he got on the grass, the noise that his boots were making on the gravel ceased, but there wasn't ANY NOISE AT ALL. You couldn't hear any noise. The boots would

have made some noise on the grass. My friend, he was very frightened. But the area that we had been in had the reputation of being haunted."

Michael's comment on his friend being frightened was fairly obvious. They were both terrified. And his explanation that he was not a good person to talk to about faeries because he had moved around a lot was offered very logically.

Much is also said about the banshee-type of disappearing person. The banshee are usually solitary women, and are either seen or heard only momentarily. This story from Simon was told sincerely:

"There is this other that lives next door to my friend, young Billy Quinn. He was very much of the school of, 'Well, that's the sort of thing my parents believed in, but I don't.' He was up in the forestry, and they were working there. I don't think he will talk about it, but as it was related he saw this figure, and I believe he saw it clearly as a figure moving fairly rapidly through the woods. He attributed to it a ghostlike feminine quality, and he attributed it to be a banshee. He took quite a bad turn, and took several days off work. As I say, he won't talk about it. But he is quite convinced that is what he saw.

"The only thing about it is, that to my knowledge, no member of his family was taken. So, whether he saw the banshee and she was going somewhere else as it were, and she wasn't meant to be seen, I don't know."

This is a firsthand report given quite recently. The farmer was absolutely convinced about it:

"I heard the banshee before the neighbour died. It was 600 or 700 yards away from here the first time, and I just heard the cry. You never see her you know. And in a split second she'd be up again by the road. She'd be down in the field for the first cry, and then she'd be up here in a split second for the second cry.

"She only goes to certain people. She follows certain families and then with some other families if anyone is about to die, a knock comes to the door the night before they die, a little knock. It is often said that a bird such as a robin taps at the window the night before."

She combs her ashen hair
And wailing congeals the air:
She is The Badhbh, [10] *her keening's never done -*
Her cloak obscures the warming sun!

The faeries are hardly restricted to land activities. Their maritime adventures are equally well known among the country folk, especially in the seaside areas and on the outer islands. The fishermen are strong believers in the unseen worlds. Despite their rugged endurance and physical strength, they are always careful not to offend the faeries. Their predilection towards belief is quietly kept, but anyone who knows them well will tell you it is there. Many a story is told about how the faeries appeared to them in some form, and how they saved someone from catastrophe, or conversely, were responsible for "taking away":

"A stranger lad came to the village long ago. He got a night's lodging the night he came, and he remained for a long time. He used to go out fishin' with the fishermen, and no one knew who he was nor where he came from.

"One night they went out, and he was with them. They went a good distance from home, as far as the foot of Ducalla Head or beyond to Rineen. The night became rough, and he - the stranger lad - told them to make haste home, that a storm was coming.

"They turned for home, and were rowing with all their might. This lad gave three rings to the captain, and told him when he saw a bad roller of a wave coming upon them to throw a ring at it. They were rowing hard on their way home. A great roller of a wave rose behind them and it would have drowned the boat if it had reached it; but the captain threw a ring at it, and it subsided. He did the same thing the second and the third time, and by then they were ashore. They came ashore safe and sound, but there was no sign of the lad. They did not know how he had gone from them, and he was not seen again. There were eighteen women widowed that night." [(37)]

Seán contributed this story of Concarr, and although it is not claimed to be about a faery being, you never know what might happen in Irish waters:

"Peculiar things happen to boat men and seafaring men, I was told by an old man - whose name was Concarr and was called Con. They owned a big fishing smack, and did a lot of trading outside Donegal bay and way down. In fact, they went sometimes down as far as Galway and on the southern side of Donegal bay. The crew was comprised of Con's brother, and his nephew, young Con.

"They were sailing somewhere outside Croagh Patrick. They had the custom then when sailing by the mountain of lowering the mainsail three times in respect for the saint. When they were comin' toward Croagh Patrick, a sudden gust of wind caught the boat, and the sail swung around. The force threw young Con overboard.

"It took the crew some time before they were able to come around again. They tried to help him into the boat. He had got a haircut like our skinheads of today - all the hair off. The father tried to grab him, but couldn't get a proper grip. The lad came up three times, and after the third time, he never came up any more.

"So, naturally the father was frantic. He lost his head altogether. Con had to lock him down below, and then he had to sail on his own to Killybegs. It was a distance of about sixty miles. When he was crossin' that particular spot - now I can't swear it was just there - the sail dipped three times without him layin' a hand on it. Miraculous. He didn't know how it happened, but it just happened. He was tellin' me often enough."

Many locals still believe that a solitary redhaired woman, if seen nearby, will bring bad luck to fishing enterprises. She is often a social isolate, and is thought to be "with the faeries". Many traditional fishermen will even today hesitate before allowing a redhaired woman on board. One of them told me this one:

"I heard a man tell that he used to hear fishing crews say that if they met a certain woman of the village any night when they were going fishing they might as well return home and go to bed that night - if the other boats in the haven were full of fish that night, they would not catch one."

When I was first enrolled in Kindergarten I told the teacher that my brother and I were adopted. Since we both had the russet-locked, green-eyed Irish colouring that was obviously in sharp contrast to that of my parents, this presumably helped me come to the conclusion that we two were from somewhere else.

There we were, the two of us with red curls and brown freckles, among a population of teutonic giants. Were we to have been transported to an Irish classroom, we would have been indistinguishable from many of the members who sat on the hard, cold benches. So, perhaps we were from somewhere else...

This invention caused my mother some embarrassment, but I think it came from my feeling that I was different - not only from them but everyone else as well. Since I also assumed that this was most likely every child's experience of himself, I concluded that there wasn't much that could be done about it.

As well as my faery granddaughter, I now have five wondrous grandsons. Three of them have colouring and facial features quite similar to my brother and me, from bright-red hair to golden red, also in contrast to expectations. Pug nosed. Green-blue eyed. Many freckles. (A fourth, a tow-headed beauty, is adopted and the fifth is still bald.) They bring fortune, not misfortune, but I'm not sure I'd let any of those energy balls on a fishing boat either.

From the mountains to the sea, an extraordinary mixture of narratives in all. Some, no doubt, are possible to explain as "natural" phenomena. However, stories like these abound in every part of rural Ireland, inviting the question: Can such extensive observation of faeries and their effects really be explained by any theory of mass delusion or ignorance?

112

XIII

The Shining Ones

*The little faeries live on love. They create faery dust, and it generates energy
within their own being.*
*They have the ability to take the love dust - the faery dust - and sprinkle it on
troubled areas, and war will be no more. It is the dust of peace and love. It
comes from their whole being.*
*They can stand there and shake it off them. Wherever it falls, those who
encounter the dust of the faeries will respond to peace and love and harmony.*

Spirit

When we investigate spirit entities from perspectives other than the
rural country folk, a somewhat different picture emerges, which adds
to the mystery and yet helps explain it at the same time. Angels and
sprites have always been recognised by the great spiritual teachings of the
world. The Seers tell us that the "Shining Ones" have always been with us. This
teaching is found everywhere, in every ancient and contemporary religion or
philosophy. The most marked characteristic of their appearance is a "brilliant
luminous radiance." The Hebrew, Christian, and Muslim religions call the
higher among them Angels and Archangels.

In ancient and medieval times, people's concept of these energies was of life-
sized, powerful beings sometimes coexisting here with us. Nymphs, dryads and
some other beings associated with the natural world were often mentioned.
Homer and Hesiod were two of numerous Greek writers who described faery
like beings, and some of the Roman writers were Virgil, Ovid, and Pliny the
Elder.

Socrates said about the sylphs that "the air is used by them as the water and the sea are by us, and the ether is to them what the air is to us". This ether did not mean the natural atmosphere of the earth, but the invisible, intangible spiritual medium then believed in.

During the Middle Ages most people continued to believe in a host of supernatural beings - angels, sprites, faeries, and the devils. The faery was a commanding entity of significant stature, to be reckoned with. Some accounts of faeries by medieval writers portrayed them in a favourable light, but many feared them, linking them with devils and evil spirits.

The sixteenth century Swiss physician Paracelsus wrote extensively and quite sympathetically for his time about the "nymphs, sylphs, pygmies, salamanders, and kindred beings". He believed in a universe in which there are an infinite number of dimensions beyond the human one and that man possesses powers and latent faculties by which it is possible for him to gradually become aware of this many-dimensional universe. That one could have talents by which he may penetrate some of these dimensional boundaries and become aware of invisible creatures was not a foreign idea to him. He thought our comparative ignorance on the subjective side of life was due mainly to our "hypnotic addiction to objectivity".

Paracelsus believed that since these beings were of subtle invisible ethers, they would be visible only at certain times when conditions were favourable. Sightings would occur only to those in rapport with their ethereal vibrations. Some Greeks apparently believed otherwise, that many nature spirits had actual "material constitutions" capable of functioning in the physical world.

According to Paracelsus, there are the airy sprites, the sylphs; the earth workers such as the gnomes; the water sprites such as the undines; and the least known of the groups, the fire spirits or the salamanders. This paradigm is still in use and although others have adopted it, he did lay a groundwork. Much of what he said can now be looked at as perhaps the wisest of the incorrect ideas of his age. Other observations of his remain valid even in this time.

He observed that, "All these creatures resemble human beings and are otherwise recognised, and yet do not belong to the human race." The elementals are elusive. "They are not seen at all times, but only rarely," and "only that we should know that they exist." Yet not only has man seen these elusive ones, he has spoken to them. He has even "lived and kept house with them".

The habitations of the nature spirits vary according to the element in which they exist. Each "race" remains confined to its own element, and they have their own food and drink, "the chemistry of which we cannot fathom". They are discreet and chaste, he tells us, and have their own laws - higher than the laws of animals, but lower than human laws.

The Divine One dresses not only us, but them. "All are under divine protection and care. He clothes and guides all creatures; not only men, but many beings we know not of. As God sent his angels to guide and guard our lives, he has also sent the elementals among us."

The Swiss physician tells us that their function is mainly that of guardians of the earth. "They know the past, present and future of humanity and often warn and guide those to whom they are attached." [38]

Contemporary metaphysical writer Manly Hall has elaborated on these categories, calling on the knowledge of other sources as well as Paracelsus. He writes that the undine functions in the invisible, spiritual essence called humid ether. Its vibratory rate is closest to the element of water. The course and the function of water are said to be under their control, and their natural habitats are those of the sea, and of the mountain lakes and waterfalls on the lands.

Of the kingdoms, the undines are depicted as the most graceful, often described as symmetrical and sensuous in form. They are often symbolised as feminine in nature. To the ancients they closely resembled human beings in appearance and size, although seem a lesser size in the smaller streams and rivers. The temperament of the undine is seen as vital, rather emotional, friendly to human life, receptive, and sympathetic.

The sylphs are the spirits of the air. They "live" hundreds of years, often attaining a thousand, never seeming to grow old. They sometimes assume human form, apparently for only short periods of time. In the majority of cases, they are no larger than humans and often considerably smaller. It has been said that sylphs have accepted human beings into their communities and have permitted them to live there for a considerable period. Paracelsus wrote of such an incident, although he said "it could not have occurred while the human stranger was in his physical body".

Sylphs' temperament is mirthful, changeable and eccentric. Intellectual, adaptable, communicators. Peculiar qualities common to men of genius are supposedly the result of the cooperation of the sylphs, but this aid also brings with it the sylphic inconsistency that accompanies this temperament.

116

The gnomes, the leprechauns, and the elves were said to contain the vibratory rate closest to material earth, having considerable power over its mineral content, and the mineral elements in the animal and the human. Traits attributed to them include energy and vitality, practicality, melancholy, thrift, and wealth in all forms.

Whimsical shape-changers, they seem to have the reputation of being both the most amiable and the most naughty of the different divisions, even to the degree of being capable of malevolent acts. Folklore, both European and Celtic, continued to support this idea to some extent.

The salamanders, the ones with the fewest legends, were seen as existing in the spiritual ether constituting the invisible fire element. Without their aid fire cannot exist, or so the medieval mystics believed. Man is unable to communicate successfully with them, because of the fiery element in which they dwell. They differ greatly in appearance, size and dignity sometimes described as small balls of light, Will-o-the-wisps, or according to Paracelsus "tongues of fire, running over the fields or peering in houses". They exert distinctive influence over all beings of fiery or tempestuous temperament. Traits associated with them include creativity, ardour, loyalty. [39]

The above categories are not commonly used in the Celtic literature, but they are apt: the hill or airy crow, - great shining ones - the banshee - could describe the sylph; the leprechaun - the brownie - the wee folk - the gnome; the immortal host of the sea - the undine; and the will-o-wisps and seldom-mentioned "fire-balls" that often act with intelligent intent - the salamander.

Seventeenth century Scottish Episcopalian minister and scholar Robert Kirk was an implicit believer in faeries. His classic text, *The Secret Commonwealth of Elves, Fauns, and Fairies* is considered one of the earliest reliable accounts of faery lore in the English language. Kirk was a Gaelic speaker, and so knowledge of the belief in the faeries and the related second sight that was still common among the Gaelic speaking Highlanders of Scotland was not only accessible to him, but part of his own heritage and belief structure.

He saw no contradiction between contact with the Secret Commonwealth and the practice of good Christianity. He was devotedly spiritual and a remarkable visionary of his time. He felt that future communication between the worlds would be a normal occurrence.

It would serve as proof of the many dimensions of reality and would counter the growth of atheism and materialism. "In the process of time we may come to converse as familiarly with those nimble and agile clans, but with greater pleasure and profit, as we do now with the Chinese and Antipodes."

Robert Kirk described the faeries thus: "The faeries are of light, changeable bodies, like those called Astral, somewhat of the nature of a condensed cloud, and best seen in twilight...their bodies of congealed air are sometimes carried aloft, while others grovel in different shapes...

"The faeries are distributed in Tribes and orders; and they have children, nurses, marriages, deaths and burials, in appearance even as we do, unless they so do for a mock show, or to prognosticate some such things that will come to be among us... (And their houses) having for light continual lamps, and fires, often seen burning without fuel..." [40]

Kirk's stance was uniquely progressive. In Scotland during the witch trials the recognition of witches as the victims of the faeries was almost commonplace. The question, whether the accused witch "hed ony conversation with the ffaryefolk" would seem to have been a stock question of witchcraft trials. Although there was some indication that a difference existed between being a witch and being someone who had a relationship with the faeries, it was definitely a risky time to be either one.

Around the beginning of the 17th century the belief in the reality of faery declined in most of the English speaking world at least, and was replaced by the belief in the mythological faery, a diminutive and harmless mutant offspring of powerful parentage.

Latham's scholarly book, *The Elizabethan Fairies*, published in 1930, concerned itself with the faeries of Shakespeare and especially with their reputed size. In talking of the faeries of *Midsummer Night's Dream* in particular, Latham tells us that whatever was homely or tangible or risky has been removed. They are diminutive, charming and quaint sprites and most importantly they differ from the faeries of tradition. Instead of appearing as "an active and powerful commonwealth", they appear instead in the role of "innocuous attendants of two literary or mythological sovereigns, Oberon and Titania".

For the first time in a recognised literary production, the faeries were made consistently good. The wickedness and devilish alliances are omitted, and "the period of their earthly materialisation is devoted to making the world happier and more beautiful, without any of the usual impositions of taboos and without any of the usual demand for worship or payment".

118

Their dignity was diminished, their dimensions reduced, their characters notably redeemed and their association with flowers and insects established. If Shakespeare had wanted to destroy an ancient belief, he succeeded. No longer did the faeries occupy "dark and mysterious portions" of the earth, no longer were they adult and substantial beings. The bard laid the groundwork for a new concept of faery.

Many reasons have been given for his emphasis on the spritely qualities of faery. If he were directly inspired, as many believe, his portrayal of faery did much to remove the fear so attached to them in his time.

There was a renewal of interest in the faery during the late eighteenth century, as a rejection of the Age of Reason. In modern times we have an emerging scientific paradigm in the realm of quantum physics that acknowledges the possibility of other dimensional realities.

In the West, the teachings of the Theosophists have been worthy preservers of the faery tradition, and are said to reflect the most contemporary findings in this field. According to the position of the non-sectarian Theosophical Society, the universe is a living entity or being, composed of countless parts and kingdoms. All the kingdoms are endowed with their own kind of energy and inhabitants with sense and minds. There are the healing angels, the building angels, the angels of music, and the angels of nature. They are widely distributed, each dwelling and working in his own element.

They are of infinite variety - and this is why the reports on them vary to such an extent. The nature spirits are responsible for the administration of nature, in carrying out the will of God. Metaphysical author Annie Besant emphasised that "the faeries and elves of legend...the charming irresponsible children of Nature, whom science has coldly relegated to the nursery" will be replaced in "their own grade of natural order by the wiser scientists of a later day". [41]

New consciousness writers consistently speak of the reality of angelic entities as well as their country cousins, the elementals. Ken Carey, whose beautiful prose has earned him an honoured reputation among the followers of the new thought, eloquently connects for us the past and the future:

"As you thank God for the people and ideas that helped to make these centuries much better than the worst they could have been, thank also the deities of sky, sun, moon and star. Thank the deities that live within the trees, that bubble forth in the springs that give you your water to drink, that ripen the wheat, the corn, the potato in the field. For all of these deities, ignored though they have been, have continued to exercise a benevolent influence and have helped to lighten for you the trauma of these past centuries."

They speak to us - and always have - in whispers, in "gentle voices" in dreams and a myriad of other ways sometimes unnoticed. Carey emphasises that we need honour and revere them. He continues:

"Though these are the same deities the Tuatha Dé Danann honoured on the shores of Killarney, the same deities that the druids thanked with their first cup of water at every bubbling forest spring, the same beings the African bushmen and Australian aborigines call upon today, they are not 'pagan' gods. They are helpful beings, essential energies, not one of which lacks consciousness. They are specific ways that God has chosen to serve you in this material world. Every time you give reverence to any one of these, you honour God." [42]

XIV

The Changeling

The midwife straight howls out, there was no hope
Of the infant's life; swaddles it in a flay'd lambskin,
As a bird hatch'd too early; makes it up
With three quarters of a face, that made it look
Like a changeling; cries out to Romelio
To have it christen'd, lest it should depart
Without that it came for.

(John Webster) [43]

There is an opinion that there are those on earth who have "come from" the elemental and devic kingdoms. If there was nothing to the concept of having "faery transmigrates" around, surely this imaginative theme would not have gained recognition. However, I discovered the idea has been around since man was first able to communicate this in some form.

Expressions are found in the world's esoteric teachings, and in all the symbolic art expressions, especially those of music and poetry. The belief that we have come here from other dimensions as well as other planetary systems is contained in the majority of current spiritual teachings. Still, these faery wanderers have been whirled around in the faery winds to a remarkable degree. They have fallen to the ground in disgrace, or have soared to the heights to hold hands with the angels. The Celtic areas such as Ireland, Wales and Scotland in particular have noted the habits, the personality traits of those designated as "in with the faeries" or "away with the faeries". This is where they came to when they were cast from out of the sea, or wafted down from the mountain, or came silently through the mists.

These voyagers more often than not have been feared, or at least held ambivalently. They were psychic, sensitive, and often quite strange, and outcast or abused.

Those differently born have often been labelled changelings, or acquire this title shortly after birth when a mysterious baby switch takes place. This term is quite familiar to those with a Celtic background, although less recognised elsewhere, if at all. Other terms such as "crossover" often refer to this exchange, and the definitions are used in a confused fashion, depending on era or locale.

Researcher Latham noted that before 1500 the faeries had been accused of bewitching babies causing them to become diseased or to die, which is a practice they continued "as long as they existed". But, as far as he could discover, there are no records in the British Isles until the middle of the 16th century of the exchange of faery children for mortal offspring which resulted in the disappearance of the human infant and the appearance of a strange and supernatural baby in its stead.

In Ireland, a changeling event usually means a particularly desirable human baby is "stolen" by the faeries and an ugly old elf is found in the crib. This mutant is the changeling. The abducted baby is generally seen to have been beautifully formed and angelic in disposition, but its replacement is quite undesirable - a cranky, temperamental, ancient-looking infant, it turns out to be. The concept is also seldom found in the Irish Celtic literature until around the 16th century, when much more of this type of folk superstition was about. Here is a typical example from Wentz:

"When she had her first child, a very strong and very pretty boy, she noticed one morning that he had been changed during the night; there was no longer the fine baby she had put to bed in the evening; there was, instead, an infant hideous to look at, greatly deformed, hunchbacked, and crooked, and of a black collar. The poor woman knew that a (faery) had entered the house during the night and had changed her child." [44]

Rarely was an infant simply abducted with no faery substitute left in its place, nor did a faery infant simply appear unannounced in a crib. It was never reported to be a desirable event from the standpoint of the humans involved. The faery baby was always an unwanted child. No one was ever pleased with a wizened, ill tempered elf.

Until this mid-century, the exchange was held to be a possibility in certain areas, always to be feared and guarded against. When this was thought to have

122

happened, the child so designated grew up with the changeling stigma and was usually considered inferior. Irish words in common usage for changeling, *fágálach* (laggard, weakling), *iarlais* (chronically ailing person), point this out.

It is possible that parents did not want to face being blamed for being unfit or irresponsible, so it was convenient to blame someone or something else for the birth of a "different" child. Whatever its origin, the myth explained away various congenital abnormalities and pathological conditions of birth and childhood. It would be particularly efficient within a social structure that insisted that "defective" children were a reflection of the parents' sins against the Church.

Mental imperfections, physical abnormalities, and deficiency diseases were thus conveniently accounted for. It was perhaps less distressing to parents to feel they were victimised by faeries than to wonder whether God was punishing them for a sin, although both concepts are dismal and conflicted. So, the convoluted changeling stories came into being.

As country man Seamus pointed out:

"There was much fear that the good children would be taken and replaced by deformed ones. The changeling myth was used as an excuse sometimes for bad rearing, or for accepting natural tragedies of birth. They said that they would never stop cryin', they were abominable. One hundred and twenty years ago a man and wife murdered a baby thought to be a changeling. It wasn't uncommon at all to hear such tales."

Michael, the retired garda from Connemara, was quite serious about all of this, not wanting to take a firm stand on the matter in one way or another, as perhaps in some way he might offend the forces of nature:

"They often brought faery children. They took human children and left faeries in their place. They'd abduct them and they would abandon a substitute which would be an old person resembling the child. They'd leave them at the spot where they took the child and those were called changelings.

"They were called that because of the change, and then the only way to get rid of the substitute or the changeling was to burn them or to threaten them with fire, until the changeling was sure that they were goin' to carry it out. Well, sometimes they would get the child back, sometimes. But not always, not always, no...

"It was often an excuse on the part of the people for things that happened they didn't want to take responsibility for. That way they didn't have to feel guilty, if the faeries did it."

Although the changeling myth is certainly not the only untruth about the faery dimension, it serves as an example of how distorted the human perception of this kingdom has become. It is not merely a convenient and sometimes humourous superstition boding no particular ill effects. Over time it has become as lethal as any prejudice can be, and carried to extremes it has resulted in painful loss of life or social isolation for the scapegoat.

A report from the Tralee Assizes, July 1826, tells of Ann Rocke, a woman of advanced age, being indicted for murder of a young child by drowning her in the river Flesk in County Kerry. The child couldn't stand, walk or speak. It was thought to be "faery-struck". The grandmother of the child had ordered the accused to bathe the child in that pool of the river where the three farms met for three consecutive days.

On the last morning the prisoner kept the child under the water too long and it drowned. The accused said, "the sin was on the grandmother and not on her", as she was just following instructions. Upon cross-examination, the accused woman said it was not done with intent to kill the child but to cure it - "to put

the faery out of it". The jury "would not be safe in convicting the prisoner", and the verdict was not guilty. [45]

Even if annihilation was not an inevitability for the changeling child, mistreatment could occur if it was thought that the faeries could be persuaded to return the human infant and take their own back with them. This is shown in the following account from Croker:

"A young woman, whose name was Mary Scannell lived with her husband not many years ago at Castle Martyr. One day in harvest-time she went with several more to help in binding up the wheat, and left the child, which she was nursing, in a corner of the field, quite safe, as she thought, wrapped up in her cloak. When her work was finished she returned to where the child was, but in the place of her own she found a thing in the cloak that was not half the size and that kept up such a crying you might have heard it a mile off.

"So Mary Scannell guessed how the case stood, and, without stop or stay, away she took it in her arms, pretending to be mighty fond of it all the while, to a wise woman. The wise woman told her in a whisper not to give it enough to eat, and to beat and pinch it without mercy, which Mary did; and just in one week after to the day, when she awoke in the morning, she found her own child lying by her side in the bed! The faery that had been put in its place did not like the usage it got from Mary, who understood how to treat it, like a sensible woman as she was, and away it went after a week's trial, and sent her own child back to her."[46]

Changelings themselves were not the only ones to be assigned inferior status. Often the mother was accused of faery dealings because of her plight. From *Legends of Kerry*:

"Although Jinny Mac Crohan had beauty to stop a band from marching, her name was ruined because she was believed to be in the faeries, and no sensible Christian man would have traffic with a faery-woman in the Kingdom of Kerry, or in any other Kingdom but as little..."

She left her daughter, "a sweet contented girleen with black hair and blue eyes" unattended while about some chore, and when she returned the child had red hair and green eyes. The "poor woman knew then that the faeries had been up to their tricks." [47]

Frequently found are the themes of changeling births, and of means that will protect the new-borns from being taken by the faery dwellers of the night. Here is a recent accounting from the Folklore archives which illustrates the often found connection that is made between mysterious lights or related signs and suspected faery activities:

"Old Tom Harpur, an old man that lived here long ago. His wife was (birthing) a child one night; and a light was seen coming up by the river and along the old lane by Furlong's till it come and lit on the window. That child was a faery as sure as you're born. He was always ill and crying. They used to say that old Tom was a faery man himself. We were looking at the light that night, and I tell you we cleared away very quick." [48]

This archive report also tells of protection. This practice was recalled by almost everyone I interviewed, and it was always and only the faeries from whom the birth-child needed to be insulated, not other types of supernaturals. Travelling people were often suspected to be linked to the faeries:

"In a room where a child is born, holy water is sprinkled all over the room and especially on the mother and around the bed to prevent the faeries from taking the child on (from) its mother.

"Some travelling women once called at a certain house and asked for a night's rest and they were allowed in for the night. That night a child was born in the house but the people of the house sprinkled holy water in the room so that the travelling women were not able to take the child; but in the morning they went off and said they were going to spend the next night in another house in Turnafulla that was some distance away so they departed. That night they went to the house they had mentioned and were also allowed in for the night. In that house also a child was born but the people did not use any holy water and in the

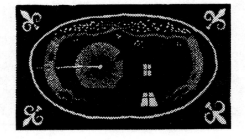

morning the woman was dead and the travelling women had gone and were never seen again." (49)

Although witch-hunting events were much less common in Ireland than elsewhere, they still occurred. Invariably witches were thought to have dealings with the faery realm, or to be changelings themselves, the grown-up variety. Sometimes a formally normal person could be "taken over" by the faeries and turned into a changeling. This real tragedy concerning an unfortunate Bridget took place only a century ago, and children in the area are said to still sing this refrain:

> *Are you a witch or a faery*
> *Or the wife of Michael Cleary?*

A recently published novel by Gábler, *The Cure*, is based on the life of Bridget and those who surrounded her, bringing this uncomfortable story to light. The narrator tells us that the violence could not be ascribed to political or partisan passions, but rather to a communal hysteria that gripped the family and neighbours of this young married woman.

Bridget was concerned about her childlessness, and paying scant attention to formal religious beliefs visited an old crone for an infertility cure. Her husband Michael did likewise, and the "cures" contribute to Bridget's declining well-being. Eventually convinced that Bridget had been supplanted by a changeling, Michael, close family and neighbours end up in murdering Bridget in an effort to remove the changeling from her, either by direct action or passive withdrawal.

Other gruesome stories in the archives contain this theme. Whether they are based on fact or imagination, they point to the prevalent fears the rural people had, and still have to some degree, concerning the mysterious, sorrowful status of a changeling.

Fortunately, the role of the changeling was not always seen as dysfunctional. Changelings could be desirable, although when this happened they were generally not referred to as changelings but the "faery boy", "one of the hill-folk", or similar designation.

The human child as portrayed in Yeats' hauntingly beautiful poem *The Stolen Child* was certainly not shunted. He would have been thought of as having faery

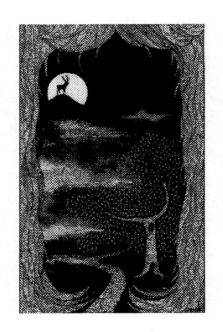

leanings, however, to be watched lest he slip away. Although quoted for so many years in so many ways, it remains a major contribution to the changeling literature. Yeats surely sensed the mystery, rather than fear, in his:

The Stolen Child

Where dips the rocky highland
Of Sleuth Wood in the lake,
There lies a leafy island
Where flapping herons wake
The drowsy water rats;
There we've hid our faery vats,
Full of berries
And of reddest stolen cherries.

Come away, O human child!
To the waters and the wild
With a faery, hand in hand,
For the world's more full of weeping than
* you can understand.*

Where the wave of moonlight glosses
The dim grey sand with light,
Far off by furthest Rosses
We foot it all the night,
Weaving olden dances,
Mingling hands and mingling glances
Till the moon has taken flight;

To and fro we leap
And chase the frothy bubbles,
While the world is full of troubles
And is anxious in its sleep.

Come away, O human child!
To the waters and the wild
With a faery, hand in hand,
For the world's more full of weeping than
* you can understand.*

Where the wandering water gushes
From the hills above GlenCar,
In pools among the rushes
That scarce could bathe a star,
We seek for slumbering trout
And whispering in their ears
Give them unquiet dreams;
Leaning softly out
From ferns that drop their tears
Over the young streams.

Come away, O human child!
To the waters and the wild
With a faery, hand in hand,
For the world's more full of weeping than
*   you can understand.*

Away with us he's going,
The solemn-eyed:
He'll hear no more the lowing
Of the calves on the warm hillside

Or the kettle on the hob
Sing peace into his breast,
Or see the brown mice bob

Round and round the oatmeal chest.
For he comes, the human child,
To the waters and the wild
With a faery, hand in hand,
From a world more full of weeping than
          he can understand. [50]

XV

The Faery Doctors

Yeats was drawn to the mystical throughout his life, and most likely was on good terms with the "good-people". He said on one occasion that no matter what one doubts, one should never doubt the faeries.

Some fifteen years before the writing of it in his little book about magical Ireland, *Celtic Twilight*, Yeats recalls falling into what seemed the "power of faery". He was coming home at night with companions when the girl he was with saw a bright light moving slowly across the road. Her brother and Yeats saw nothing until they had walked about for some time along the edge of the river and down a narrow lane to some fields where there was the remains of a church. It was covered with ivy, and scattered about were other foundations where a town once was.

They stood for some few minutes, looking over the fields full of stones and brambles and elder bushes, when Yeats saw a small bright light on the horizon, mounting slowly towards the sky, then other faint lights for a minute or two, and at last he saw a "bright flame like the flame of a torch moving rapidly over the river. We saw it all in such a dream, and it seems all so unreal, that I have never written of it until now, and hardly ever spoken of it." He felt that perhaps his recollections of things must be untrustworthy when "the sense of reality was weakened". [51]

Also in Celtic Twilight is the account of a woman who was asked to recall a regular faery visitor her mother was known to have. They called her the Wee Woman. Is she a faery? A changeling? A real person who some can see and some can't? The story condensed:

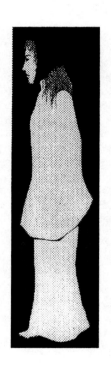

"I was a bit of a girl at the time...but I mind her as well as if I saw her there now!...It was a grey cloak she had on, with a green cashmere skirt and a black silk handkerchief tied round her head, like the country women did use to wear in them times...She was bigger than many a one, and yet not tall as you would say. She was like a woman about thirty, brown-haired and round in the face...and she never was married, and she never would take any man...maybe one of their own people that had been took off before she grew to her full height, and for that she was always following us and warning and foretelling...

"It was a thin sort of shawl she had about her in summer, and a cloak about her in winter; and many and many a time she came, and always it was good advice she was giving to my mother, and warning her what not to do if she would have good luck. There was none of the other children of us ever seen her unless me; but I used to be glad when I seen her coming up the burn, and would run out and catch her by the hand and the cloak, and call to my mother, 'Here's the Wee Woman.'

"No man body ever seen her. My father used to be wanting to, and was angry with my mother and me, thinking we were telling lies and talking foolish like. And so one day when she had come, and was sitting by the fireside talking to my mother, I slips out to the field where he was digging. 'Come up,' says I, 'if ye want to see her. She's sitting at the fireside now, talking to mother.' So in he comes with me and looks round angry like and sees nothing, and he up with a broom that was near hand and hits me a crig with it. 'Take that now!' says he, 'for making a fool of me!' And away with him as fast as he could, and queer and angry with me.

"The Wee Woman says to me then, 'Ye got that now for bringing people to see me. No man body ever seen me, and none ever will.'" (52)

Although this particular man body apparently never did see her, at a later date they had some sort of altercation. He was reported to have come into the house "all trembling like" declaring, "Don't let me hear you say another word of our Wee Woman. I have got enough of her this time."

Another that was "running with the faeries" would certainly have been Mary Bryne. This story was told to me by the folk collector Seán, after I asked him whether he ever came across anyone who was considered to be in cahoots with "them".

"I have indeed," was his emphatic reply. Then he told me this story and he did not doubt that she saw her faeries:

"I worked with a woman who lived in Malin Beg. It is on the tail end of the peninsula, west of Teelin. Have you been to Malin Beg, and have you seen the silver strand below?

"Well, hers was the last house in the town land. She was a Mary Byrne. She had a lot of chickens and ducks and all the rest of it. They had potatoes and corn and other vegetables just in front of the house. So, to get the chickens away from causing destruction they built a wee house for them, down just over the silver strand.

"In the summertime Mary was up early morning, about six. She would go down to the strand to keep the chickens. She told me more than once when she looked in the silver strand the faeries were playin' all about. She would describe for me their colours, the bright colours of their clothes they wore. She'd always describe to me the ball they had. It was very small, not any bigger than that (about 2 inches in diameter). She said that and as soon as they'd see her, they'd go away just like that. She believed in them, she did. Some were like that, in those parts."

The so-called faery doctors in Ireland were often much in demand, and their present day counterparts - healers of diverse talents - hold positions of quiet prestige in the communities. These faery physicians of old were often females. Old women, especially, are considered to have peculiar mystical and supernatural powers in that they have a knowledge of herbs, charms and incantations transmitted by tradition through many generations.

136

Their knowledge of herbs reputedly gave them power "over all disease", Lady Wilde tells us. The rurals had much more faith in these doctors than "in any dispensary doctor that ever practised amongst them".

Apparently they never revealed the nature of the herbs, preferring to gather them at night. It was sometimes thought that these doctors were stolen when they were young and beautiful, but returned as old and ugly. The compensation was that they were taught all the faery secrets and the magical mystery that lie in herbs. The women became all-powerful - "these faery women had a knowledge of all things through the power of divination they learned from the faeries".

Biddy Early, one of the most famous or infamous of the female doctors in Ireland, was a nineteenth century "wise woman" or *bean feasa*[11] of County Clare, and her legend is still alive and vigorous throughout Western Ireland. Biddy was a controversial figure. Yeats called her "the wisest of wise women", but enemies saw her a consort of the devil. This story collected by writer Lenihan is given as proof that she was "one of them":

"There was a house over in the village an' there was a little shed there one time at the west end o' the house, a shed with a galvanised roof. An' I never saw it only with the galvanised thrown up on it. 'Twouldn't be nailed at all. The wind might knock it an 'twould be thrown up simple again. 'Twas never kept in any repair, that oul' shed. But, when they used to buy pigs an' put 'em in there, they'd be found dead, black. Anyhow, a few rounds o' them died an' the man who owned it, he said he'd go out to Biddy. And he did. He told her the story.

"'Well,' she says, 'that's our path at the end of that house. An' I'm sorry,' she says, 'that your pigs had to die. But I'll tell you what you'll do. Never put a pig there again. Make another little house on the other side o' the yard, or anywhere at all, an' the ones you'll put in it'll make up for the ones that died.'

"And they did. They throve the finest, the next set o' pigs or two that was put in the new building. But never again was there a hand left to that oul' shed." [53]

That Biddy called the path "ours" was the hint that she was indeed "in the faeries". Most of the information concerning her has been taken from as conservative and first-hand sources as is possible, but many wild tales exist about her. Some accounts were from the inhabitants of her village who knew her personally, as well as several of her great-granddaughters - "charming and well-educated ladies" all.

From her early childhood she showed clearly that she was fey to a remarkable degree. She talked of seeing and even of playing with elemental beings with the same casual assurance that any other child would have in speaking of playing with a puppy or a kitten.

It was said that her mother would ask her where she had been when Biddy didn't complete an errand, and the answer would be, "Playing with 'them'." The neighbours used to shake their head and say, "She's a strange wan entirely", or "Is she one of 'them'?".

The earlier part of her life followed in some ways the normal course of the lives of the "wise women". Biddy acquired knowledge of herbal and other lore handed down from generation to generation, but also had an early knowledge of their medicinal and other occult properties from the earth folk. She knew where to look for a particular wild plant, and her reputation as a healer or white witch inevitably spread from her parish to surrounding parishes, and followed eventually to most of the counties of western Ireland.

As she grew older her psychic gifts developed even more acutely. She had an uncanny power of telling the future, and "a spirit-given healing touch lay within her magnetic-finger". It was said that, "Biddy had this type of second sight whereby she knew the caller, and what the trouble was, and she was aware of the outcome..."

Not surprisingly, curing and foretelling together with the drinking and card-playing that Biddy's husbands were almost equally famous for did not find favour with the local Catholic clergy who openly spoke out against her deeds and words. Biddy was lax in observance of the duties demanded by the Catholic church, even though her three marriages always took place in church with a proper ceremony. All of her husbands died, their deaths most likely accelerated by fondness for alcohol. She accepted no payment as was the custom with most practitioners of magic healing, but gladly welcomed gifts, and the local poteen was a not atypical offering.

Tales of the existence of faery doctors in the rural areas continue well past Biddy's and the 19th century time. Joseph pointed out the doctor's house on our hike up Knockalla mountain: "That old house there. They called him the doctor. He could cure animals, and he could cure people. They used to call them rubbin' doctors - they'd make up different rubs and things. They said he was away with the faeries, too. He could make his own medicine, all sorts of mixtures. Aye, I heard that many a time. The faeries would tell him how to do these jobs."

Another faery-doctor or "bone-setter" who was "impregnated by some faery influence" was named Moll Anthony. Her reputation as a possessor of supernatural knowledge and divination drew crowds of distant visitors to her daily and from the most remote parts of Ireland. This wise woman made as much as the accomplished doctors in the area it was pointed out. Another faery-doctor was called Paddy the Dash, and he was thought to hold friendly communication with the "good people", for his cottage adjoined one of their raths.

One story from the archives tells of a certain young boy who seemed to be quite ill. The faery man was consulted after other attempts at cure were unsuccessful, a not uncommon practice. But after consultation, the healer said he couldn't cure the boy because he had been substituted by an old faery. Yet the boy could be saved from death if he were to be "seen in the meadow and spoken to". This seemed an impossibility to the parents, as the lad in question was confined in bed this whole time, dying and too weak to be anywhere but there.

The next day, however, the wife saw the lad, or more accurately his double, in the field but did not speak to him out of fear. Later she told her husband of this sighting, and following the advice of the healer they returned to the meadow to speak to the boy-apparition, but it or he had vanished. The bed-ridden boy subsequently died. As difficult as some of these stories are to convey, they are not atypical.

Another archive story illustrates a moral twist. It seemed that a girl made fun of her cousin's ability to step-dance, as she was not as agile as this girl. The girl then became increasingly troubled with eye affliction and pain. Her mother stayed up with her several nights and took her to several doctors, but they couldn't find anything wrong. The narrator, her brother, tells the story:

"My mother didn't know what to do at all, because my sister was almost blind and she couldn't get any cure. There was a man living over in Keel and his name was Diarmuid Foley. This man used to be with the faeries every night. So my mother told him about my sister's eyes, but he said that he should see the little girl first before he could give her any cure.

"Diarmuid said that he found out from the faeries that her daughter was laughing and making fun of her own cousin. But the 'Brown Woman' from the fort threw a fist of dirt in her eyes, and he didn't know if he could cure her or not 'til he saw her.

"My mother told him to come up to the house and my little sister was in bed when Diarmuid examined her. He told my mother that she could be cured. He told my mother, that she should pay 'a round' (tithe) for her at a place called Manus, near Castlemain.

"The following day my mother took my sister to Manus and they paid the round, and in a few days time her eyes got well, but one of her eyes was weak in the sight after. She went to America when she got old." [54]

Told to Seán, this happy version of a meeting with a faery-healer took place at the Faery Well in Doochary, only a few miles from my first cottage in Gweebarra:

"There is a little well in the town land of Doochary on the left-hand side of the road going to Commeen. The local people call it Sorcha's Well. There was an old woman in the district by the name of Peggy Bhrocach (Pockmarked Peggy). She was a wizened little person, but even so, the neighbours had a great regard and respect for her. She was in great demand in her time as a midwife, and because of her calling she was very good with children.

"There was a poor man here in Doochary whose wife died, leaving a family of young children, and Peggy come to take care of them. There was one little boy who was not as strong as the rest. A rash broke out on his skin, and there was no peace to be had with him day or night.

"One day Peggy was out and had the little boy by the hand. He was very fretful and continually whining and crying. She tried every way she could to soothe him, but it was of no avail. She was sitting by the edge of the road when finally she saw a wee red-haired man coming down the hill towards her.

"He reached her, and although she had never seen him before she began to converse with him. He noticed the way the child was and asked her what was wrong with him. She told him, 'Well, if you follow my advice now,' said the wee red-haired man, 'there won't be a ha'p'orth wrong with the child this time tomorrow.'

"'Musha,' said Peggy, 'I will do any reasonable thing that would give relief to the child.'

"'Well,' said the red-haired man, 'go over to that wood and go in by the edge of the wood by the left-hand side of the road as you go east, and you will come to a small well by a rock. Wash the child in the water from that well, but for all you ever saw do not let one drop of it that falls from the child get into the well again. I promise you anything you like that it will not be long until your child is cured.'

"Peggy took the child, walked across the bridge, and when she reached the edge of the wood she searched until she found the little well. She did as the wee red-haired man had told her and no sooner had she washed the child with the water than the rash fell off in flakes. From that day until the day he died as a worn wasted old man no speck of the rash came out on his skin.

"The fame of the virtues of this well spread so that there was no one with any complaint at all that did not visit it." [55]

As well as being bone-setters and herbalists of repute, those in the faery ways have been equally known for their other psychic abilities, quite often foretelling. A recent archive account tells of the psychic Smith from County Sligo:

"Ushen't they tell this wan round here about Pether the Smith, sure I mind well hearin' ould Thomas Moran the shoemaker narratin' it in this very house. Ye know Pether was a great friend o' the Good-peoples, they ushed to take him for many aride over the counthry durin' the night, an' have him back agin next morning an' they gave him a special power for himsel' in the line o' smith work.

"It was always said round here, that Micky, that was his brother, was very good, but anything that Micky wasn't able to do Pether did it for him. An' wan day it's said a man come in to Micky, an he asked him to do a rather awkward job for him wit a bit o' iron. Micky took the piece, an' he looked at it all over, an' heted it in the fire, an' done his besht to make a job o' it, but it seems, it failed him, because he jusht left down the piece o' iron on the anvil, an' walked out.

"Pether, who was lyin' in the room was, every wan thought, sound ashleep. The minnit Micky went out in the dune, up he got and down to the forge wit him, an' he got at the bit o' iron, an' he had a job made out o' it while yid be winkin'.

"The man who owned the piece o' iron went out to tell Micky that the job was done, an' if he didn't find him cryin' for all he was worth an' lamentin' that he washn't able ta do it. Pether when he came in only laughed at him, an' tould him, that he should be on better terms wit the Good-people, an' that they'd help him."[56]

If I'd been a child in Ireland, I might have been accused of being "away with the faeries", much like some of these. When I wasn't being supervised too strictly, I would go to hideaways in the woods, usually on or by the beach. I would often have to hike some considerable distances to my secluded retreats - scattered as they were throughout the scenes of my youth. They were characterised by a particularly notable private wild beauty - usually being a small pond or lake, a fern grotto, or the like. There I would sit, or amble around, or look into the water. Did I see faery? Not that I recall. Yet I sensed their presence. It is quite easy for a child to step out of time and space, and become at one. To lose the sense of being separate, of being bound in the body. So natural.

My friend Margarita and I periodically staged an outdoor ritual in our playtime together. The location of this ceremonial was fixed and not difficult to access, as it was a large natural hillside and meadow leading to a Pacific Northwest beach next to my house. It was such a modest ceremony - we had cleared a small space at the back of an abandoned stone wall where we placed an old iron pot we had found on the beach and decorated around it with pebbles and shells. We filled this simply shaped vessel with spring water and placed 'offerings' of flower petals, leaves, and other beautiful findings from the wild garden within it. Then we would become still for quite awhile, perhaps even meditative.

We did not call it a ritual, it was just the "thing". We did not call it a sanctuary - rather just the "place". The contents of the kettle were referred to as 'our soup', but we never pretended to partake of it - it was just an identifying word. We really knew nothing of religious ceremony in this life. Was it a recall of a time of ancient celebration we were acting out?

XVI

Crossing Over

From a mystical point of view, "crossing over" is seen to be for some purpose, such as liaison work, or for the soul's desire. The idea presupposes a recognition of the fact of eternal life, and suggests that transmigration from these other kingdoms is possible.

Generally included in this framework is the idea that certain celestial orders came here, and continue to come, as teachers. Their curriculum is simple. Man and woman are the divine sons and daughters of God. Because they have forgotten this fact, the celestial ones are here to assist them on their journey home.

According to the Theosophical view, to be able to serve in this capacity as teachers, they had to give up their natural status, "descend and take up their abode on our Globe for aeons and aeons in order to impart these qualities". This elective mission of the "Fiery Angels" whose natural condition was "Knowledge and Love" has been misinterpreted by some theologies into a statement that the "Rebel Angels" were cast out of Heaven.

According to their teachings, man is evolving along one evolutionary line and the nature spirits along another line. These spirits are to angels as the animal kingdom stands to man.

The systems are generally thought to keep to their own lines of evolution and do not normally change streams while they are in them, having an evolutionary plan of their own that they usually adhere to.

This position states that not only did we work with the nature spirits on this planet in the past, we shall do so even to a greater extent in the golden future to come. We are responding to a natural, evolutionary force that works for co-operation between angelhood and humanity.

According to metaphysical author Annie Besant, all over the world there presently are people who "hold the secret that will put them in touch with elementals of one kind or another".

Certainly this has been covertly true in Ireland, but it has rarely been acknowledged to be the case. The issue of intermarriage between faery beings or supernaturals and humans is a theme that still runs consistently through the Celtic literature. An example of such a relationship is told by a storyteller from County Kerry:

"As a man was walking along the strand of Glenbeigh, he saw a mermaid sitting on a rock combing her hair. He stole over to where she was and seeing a little cap near her he took it, and the mermaid, looking around for her cap could not find it. By losing this cap she had also lost her power to return to the sea.

"The man then brought her home and married her. They lived happily together with their children for a long time until one day the man was cleaning the loft in which he kept his fishing tackle, he threw down the mermaid's cap. The minute she saw it she grabbed at it and off with her back to the sea.

"Her husband and children were all very lonely after her." (57)

Another variation, told by Seán Ó hEochaidh, where he discusses the fate of the children with casual realism:

"And the story had it that she used to come back now and then and that she used to comb their heads and wash them and that she would go back again whenever she found out that her husband was out at sea or fishing, that was the time she used to come and look after the children.

"As far as the children go, it was said that every single one of them was fair-haired, of the three youngsters, but I never heard what became of them later on, and I cannot honestly say that I have heard that anybody, anybody in the locality, had anything to do with the mermaid after that." (58)

Spirit explained that there were (and still are) some beings who have "freshly come from the other side". They have maintained an awareness of who they are, and what they came to do. This difference in awareness of the two partners is considered an intermarriage. These particular people are actually in human form, but have the ability to travel interdimensionally, as they have not lost the memory of how to do this. So, from this vantage point the legends would have literal as well as metaphorical validity.

For the most part, however, the faery people have lost this talent and are normal human beings who have varying degrees of "recollection" of their unusual ancestral roots. "They could forget that this cycle is temporary and is eternally connected to Spirit. After a certain amount of allowed time, those who were too identified with the human form lost their evolvement, and went back to the faery kingdom."

The plan had its difficulties, it seems. Not a sure thing. Some of these folks may be shipped back to the faery kingdom. What does that mean? Was it like flunking out of school? Would all those translucent folks be disappointed at those who failed?

Since Spirit has consistently identified me as one of these changeling sisters, I need to accept this as a possibility. The ensuing responsibility has certainly acted as an incentive, but a very difficult one to share with anyone. On this issue, no one has left a record before me.

The nature spirit people need not suffer from the bad press that has often been their lot. Yet, it is easy to get lost here. Perhaps adjustment will be easier in the future, when those from the nature kingdoms know themselves better. The work that is being done now will make it possible for future generations to find the way easier than we have done.

This merry band of "cross-overs" have certain personality traits - or perhaps better-stated as attitudes - in common. In general, Spirit has described them as extremely social people, networkers. They have fewer downs than ups, a freeness about them, a lightness, a sense of humour, a sparkling energy. They tend to be forgetful - when whatever they were doing is no longer compelling, they just willingly go on to the next thing.

The faery people in particular have even a closer cluster of similar attitudes, according to Spirit; as do the others from their respective realms - the gnomes or little people, as an example. The faery kin are described as the most fey of the elementals. They are naturally interested in whimsy, poetry, fancy, beauty in their surroundings, flowers, nature and the like. Such a composite sounds not unlike a generic faery. Yet, I continue to add my own similar observations - including being aware of the downside of such a profile.

To further astonish me, Spirit told me that I would begin to meet with recognition those from the nature spirit realms at a fairly consistent rate - the faery people in particular. This would be quite a feat, since there are only a relative few of the faery people around - only a small group operates with some success in this dimension.

Spirit stated many times that less than half of the 5,000 who originally "came over" specifically from the faery kingdom are still around to carry out their liaison function. Of this approximate 2,000 who have "constitutionally" been able to remain here, only 157 have a sound idea of their identity. (Those "descended" from the other nature spirit or elemental realms are more numerous.)

Although it was a great relief to find out others besides myself had been tapped for this work, I thought the statistical chance of these meetings happening would be highly improbable. Again, I was wrong. To date, I have met or know of about twenty of my kin, and while this number represents a scant one percent of the 2,000, it is remarkable for this to happen in a world-wide population. Highly sceptical of this information at first, I am learning there is truth to it.

Of the handful of the faery kin I have become personally acquainted with, I could say a few words. One common observation is we are all quite tiny and small-boned, I being the tallest of the group at 5 feet 2 inches - kind of "airy" looking. One could hardly state that this height requirement be a pre-requisite for entry to this strange assembly, but there may be a truth to it.

An example of this synchronisation follows. While attending a consciousness workshop in Hawaii in the spring of 1992 I met up with Jenny from Australia, whom I had met briefly before in California. I explained to her that I was on my way to Australia, as I was on my annual pass as a privileged airline employee's mother.

Afterwards Jenny came up to me and said, "Come and stay with me. I have someone I would love you to meet. His name is Kinsley Jarrett and he lives only a few miles from me. He is certainly one of the faery people. He is delightful, but has been somewhat isolated there in the rain forest...a little reluctant to share."

I told her, "I can understand his reluctance. I would love to meet him. I was actually just going to write him, just cold. You see, I just finished reading Michael Road's book, *Journey into Nature*, a story of Michael's journeys into the otherworlds. Kinsley Jarrett is the artist who depicted a devic presence on the cover of this book, and Roads mentioned him in his text. I was intrigued by him. So now, I have a direct contact instead."

I subsequently met up with Kinsley, and he is certainly one who epitomises this light-hearted energy. His family is grown, and he lives with his gracious wife along Australia's gold coast in a romantic house not far from the beach. A very small man, he is perfectly proportioned, lithe and masculine in his movements. One truly gets the impression that he could fly if he wished. When I think of him, he is always in movement.

His good nature was infectious, and he appeared delighted to have someone to talk to who could be supportive. When he wasn't talking he was drawing, or playing the organ with expertise, or walking through the lush jungle surrounding his house.

"My mates, they think I've gone off the edge. My mates at work. They don't say so, but that is my guess. You know what I was doing for a living? Commercials, drawing commercials. Living in an apartment in downtown Sydney. Now, I'm up at dawn, and armed with my sketch pad, wandering through the woods drawing faeries."

Shortly after Kinsley retired he begun to have direct and sometimes even visible contact with sources of higher consciousness:

"When this first started happening, I would go out in the forest, quiet myself, and enter into a state of meditation. Nothing particular happened in the beginning, but I just felt an intuition to do what I was doing.

"I love the forest, the beach. There is such a sense of the old ones here, the Aborigine. Then slowly at first, and more clearly afterwards, I would actually see these forms. It was like a series, though. When it was done, it was done."

Kinsley went on to explain rather precisely how this happened to him, using his experiences in creating his book, *Visions of the Ascended Masters*, which had been recently published. It is a series of sixteen sketches of such illuminata as Master Jesus, Master Lord Buddha, and Master Maha Chohan as well as other perhaps lesser known "ascended masters".

According to esoteric theory, these masters are alive and well and are guiding us in whatever ways we will let them towards our own inevitable movement into enlightenment. Kinsley, however, had not come about knowledge of this group through reading metaphysical literature.

"No, it comes to me directly. I'm just not a good reader. What happened when I received these impressions, is that I would go out in the forest and wait. It all happened in a few weeks. I would feel guided to go and bring my sketch pad. And then one by one, these impressions would come to me. Like they would zoom in on a bubble, and then stay in place until I finished".

He explained that these bubble forms would accommodate him as he drew them, and would stay visible until he finished. Then, the forms would be gone. After that, he would go into meditation and he would receive a message. The messages are contained in the text in his book. Of the Master Serapis, he wrote in part that he was encouraging and stimulating creative ideas in the realms of artistic and musical work:

"This Master also dispenses energies to those who work harmoniously with Nature and the healing of the Earth's environment. Being Master of the Devic Kingdom, Serapis helps those who are spiritually attuned to Nature, for they receive help in unveiling previously unseen life forms in dimensions within such environments." [59]

It was a privilege to see an unpublished collection of drawings of nature beings which Kinsley has met in the forest in similar fashion. The great god Pan appeared to him on occasion, not only in meditation, but he was really there, and sat calmly on a stump while Kinsley sketched him. Pan's message to him was:

"I come in love as an expression of The Divine Source within a dimension of Nature existing parallel to yours. In my reality, I am a vortex of the light and energy that permeates all life forms."

Susan D'Aoust is also one of the "changelings" of "little people" origin. She is not specifically attuned to the faery genre, but rather the elfin energy, the gnome, the leprechaun. These people tend to be more solid, both in size and build - one could easily say more "earthy types".

Susan lives in a remote farm in Idaho which is nestled in a valley circled by tall, silent mountains. She is a published author, having already two well-received novels to her credit. Set in Alaska, *Longshadows* is the one she feels most exemplifies the earth energy. Susan seems quite naturally attuned to the nature spirit kingdoms. She wrote to me, saying:

"I was taken with your notes on the personality of the elementals. It fits me to a big T and so many of those characteristics (of sensitivity) are things I have struggled to eradicate or balance most of my life."

This author perceives a difference in people who come from the "faery clan" as opposed to those of the "leprechaun clan" in that she believes herself to be of a slightly denser energy than I. She does not feel "faery" but does feel "little people", however "weird and crazy that may seem to others." And I feel "faery" but not so much "little people".

Susan "feels energy" much more than most of the people she knows, and has always had difficulty not taking on other people's pain and trying to make them well by absorbing it into her consciousness.

I have consistently observed among the faery and elfin types an affinity for and interest in working with one's natural psychic abilities. Such aptitudes are hardly exclusive with them, but they demonstrate a natural trust in the intuitive to a remarkable degree.

Joseph of the Fanad peninsula explains and demonstrates these states to us as well as anyone, and gives us a hint, that in Ireland at least, they may be passed down from generation to generation.

Joseph told me that not only did his grandfather regularly see the faeries, but he was "knowing" in other ways too. It appears he passed on the gift of second sight to all succeeding generations. Joseph describes his father as "a man who used to see a lot of ghosts and things like that". One time his father was cutting peat up at Knockalla Mountain and came back home to announce that "there is somebody dead that belonged to him". So, "they wondered to hear that", but quite soon the local postman came with a wire from America to say that his father's sister had died.

On another occasion Joseph was sitting in his young daughter's room and a book "flew across the room" of its own accord. This daughter, a beauty now grown, briefly confided to me that the mechanical toys in her room used to "turn themselves on" during that period. Joseph explained later that this happened quite often, when the family was all asleep. Her room was a small partition next to his and his wife's room, so they could observe this accurately, he emphasised. Joseph explained his psychic gifts:

"I don't know how to explain this but I be very, very fast in chancin' (sensing) something. If there is something happening or something wrong I will be very, very fast with it. I could see it for miles from a far off distance.

"Well, let's say that I was friendly with somebody over the road there, and some slight upset between me and them would occur. I would have no reason to know that there was a bad feeling, but then I would know that straight away.

"There are different things as well that you know in advance. Something tells you, but you can't describe it very well. But for some reason or other, the feeling would come onto me, and I would be 100% right every time. You would always wonder as to how you would know that.

"Sometimes I'll know what people are thinking in a crowd. I'll nearly know what they are going to say in advance, but why I know that I can't tell you. It's one of those things you'd be explaining better. Aye, I do a lot of thinking..."

XVII

Building Bridges

My visit to Patrick Francis illustrates how quickly an Irish psychic picked up on the idea of intuition and its connection to the unseen realms. He had never met me, nor did he know anything about me before our visit.

It was a blustery and wet, wet day in Dublin when I set out for my appointment on Grattan Street with Patrick, who is a beacon light in the new consciousness movement in Ireland. Patrick is a psychic counsellor, and author of several books on higher consciousness. I had made an appointment with him via a mutual friend as I wished to make his acquaintance, and to perhaps get some advice on the publishing of the book.

Since it was raining with serious intent, I had put my umbrella to use, an unfamiliar object to a Californian. Dubliners walk around looking quite a bit like colourful toadstools with legs when it rains. Thousands of umbrellas of all shapes and sizes in full bloom.

Some of these mobile mushrooms are courteous, but others walk as if they were solitary beings in open space. Somehow, like the traffic, it all works. At first I was holding my umbrella higher above the other ones, as it was quite large and I thought I might impale someone with its spokes. However, with a gust of wind I nearly was airborne, and rather than appear as Mary Poppins sailing to my appointment, I discontinued this procedure.

I then tried to walk with my umbrella down, but the wind treated this procedure with even more severity, almost turning the object inside out. There were umbrellas with fatal casualties abandoned in the rubbish bins here and there, so I was appreciative of mishaps. Yet, I witnessed none.

Grattan Street is removed from the busy part of the city, but my directions were clear. When I arrived at what I thought was my destination, I asked for directions from a serious looking young woman entering an office. She admitted that she did not even know the name of her own street. "But isn't it Grafton Street that you might be wanting? It is down the road quite a piece, and you have sure gone out of your way gettin' there if that's where you wanted to go. But I can show you how to get there."

I enunciated clearly that it was Grattan Street I wanted. "But are you sure it isn't Grafton Street you'd be wantin'? That's a popular place. I can show you..."

But, that glamourous boulevard, very much a tourist attraction, was not my destination that day. The man standing under the veranda in the next building was witnessing our conversation with interest, and confirmed to me that this was indeed Grattan - from the beginning all the way down to the end. "Now, if you be tellin' me the name of who you are visitin', maybe I can show you just where they live. Is it an apartment you are lookin' for ...?"

I knew too well that it was an invitation for me to detail clearly what my business was, and who it was with. Had I told him I was an American living in Donegal studying the faeries, and was about to visit a psychic who had his office across the street, he would have stayed with me and listened for an hour. Most likely he would have given me a good story or two. Perhaps he would have relatives or friends somewhere in Donegal. Although I was in metropolitan Dublin, in this particular block at least, I was still very much in Ireland.

He did stay with me until we had located the correct building, and waved a friendly good-bye as I entered the office. Patrick lived up to his reputation of being a wise gentleman. Tall, greying and lithe, he speaks gently. He listened to his inner wisdom and somewhat confirmed what Spirit had told me. His guidance told him right away that I had come here to "build a bridge" to the unseen worlds. I was a writer in this capacity, and my work was meant to be "light-hearted and humourous" rather than sombre or serious.

"People need to learn that spirituality is meant to be a joyful experience. The only reality is consciousness, which in its aware state is joy, happiness, bliss, all included in love."

Patrick stressed that communication between the non-physical and physical worlds is normal rather than abnormal, and that the difficulties related to time and space are a feature of earth life only. He emphasised the sensitivity possessed by those "who have incarnated from the devic worlds to help in the transition". Patrick maintained that although this sensitivity can illuminate feelings and artistic forms, such people are vulnerable and easily hurt.

"Life is difficult for you in this density...you are not used to it. You have always lived in two worlds at the same time..."

Such thoughts have been confirmed by the faery people I have talked to. Patrick said, "Do not turn down any leads. Follow them all." Also, I might not think of retiring for awhile, for my work was just beginning.

Perhaps it began a little before the beginning, when I wasn't so aware. It was during the height of the Vietnam protest movement in America in the early 1970's. My three teen-age daughters and I were sitting in a health-food restaurant-bookstore in Mendocino, California. The family would spend summers there.

I was reading quietly to them of a man named Roc and his adventures with nature spirits, as described in the just published *The Findhorn Garden*. At first the book was not well known outside of a small circle, and even within that group it was considered a delightfully heretical book.

I felt I must be discreet about discussing its contents so as not to be classified as too odd. This would actually have been an achievement of sorts, considering the gathering in that seaside cafe.

My children, considerably more conservative than both the protesters and I, were rather embarrassed by me lest a potential boyfriend might overhear their mother speaking of even imaginary, let alone real, elfin beings.

I was abundantly fascinated by the book, particularly by Roc's meeting with a faun in the Edinburgh Botanical gardens. It was his habit to stroll in that tranquil setting, but he never expected to see this incredible sight that memorable sunny afternoon:

"I saw something moving from the corner of my eye, something that distracted me. I looked and saw a figure dancing around a tree some twenty-five yards away. And then I looked again. It was quite startling. It was a beautiful figure about three feet tall."

Not surprisingly, he conjectured that the figure was made up. A hallucination. Yet it seemed as real as the other people who were also walking in the park, although they apparently could not see the faun. Roc wasn't sure that he was seeing him with his physical eyes, though when he closed them the boyish creature was not there. After tangling with and dismissing his rationalising, he fortunately chose to enjoy his experience:

"He could not be - there was something about him that was not human. Although he was moving, I could see shaggy legs and cloven hooves, pointed chin and ears, and the two little horns on his forehead. His eyes seemed brown and dark, and his skin was a light honey colour, very much like the colour of the trees. He was naked, but his legs were covered with fine hair. If he were a real boy, I would have said he was ten or eleven years old. But he was not a real boy."

The faun, dancing around the tree, moving his arms about, prancing, came to survey Roc, he being surprised that Roc could "see" him. The story goes that the Faun, by name of Kurmos, accompanied Roc back to his flat, eventually returning to his own dimension by simply vanishing.

I remember wanting to simply pack my bags and go to Findhorn, to experience Kurmos for myself and to work with him. Such an idea did not fit into my life-style nor my concept of myself: To simply abandon all and sit under a tree in northern Scotland to wait for an elf to show up. It was strange. Yet, so very quietly reminiscent. Of what, I knew not. Nor could I have guessed then that nearly twenty years of waiting lay "in front of me" before I would find myself not in Scotland but in neighbouring Ireland doing just what I had wanted so fleetingly to do then.

At one time Findhorn was a partially protected unimpressive patch of ground composed mainly of sand and gravel, continually swept by gale-force winds and rain - a place where most would be glad to explain that nothing could grow there except a few leaf and root crops. Not unlike Donegal. Yet this was where the founders of Findhorn - Peter and Eileen Caddy and Dorothy Maclean - were guided by higher wisdom to plant their garden.

Spirit gave instructions, and when they stayed in the flow "miracles" occurred daily. Needed materials showed up, and the garden prospered. In this sandy wasteland a garden sprung. It produced several varieties of lettuces and cabbages, onions and their relatives, celery, carrots, parsnips, swedes, turnips, artichokes, kohlrabi, herbs, and potatoes. Many were of initial giant size, and were full of the loving vibrations they were constantly told to express and nurture.

The over-guiding principle of the community, which now has attracted international attention, is that divine grace is stimulating the change in human consciousness.

A musician, a mathematician, and a scientist, Roc lived in a 150-year-old drawing room flat in Edinburgh from his twenties until his death in his late seventies, but also apparently lived alone in the forest for some time. An explorer of consciousness, his flat was crammed with seven thousand books which he found of particular interest over his lifetime.

An admirer of his said of him, "He had the innocence of the ancients, not of youth. When he speaks to you he is wandering in areas of his mind which you don't have a hint of."

As well as his initial meeting with Kurmos, Roc continued to have encounters with nature spirits and the great god Pan, seeing and sensing them at times with his particular gift of sight. The main reason for his continuing communication with the nature spirit realm was the contribution it made to the work in the Findhorn Garden and its development. By consciously linking with the Nature Spirits, beneficial knowledge could be received that was complementary to their already established link with the Devic World. These pioneers were establishing contact and cooperation between three kingdoms at Findhorn: the Devas, Nature, and Man. This became the aim of the Garden.

Roc had a gift that most of us still need to develop, our "latent seership". Although the nature spirits at the Findhorn gardens are reported to be seen on occasion by some, to my knowledge, no one since Roc has had his acute sight.

Many continue to work in the gardens, communicating with the nature forces "with the third eye".

Roc explained that the nature spirits work with the etheric body of a plant, the archetype, and are able to influence its growth and development by their will. Builders, to some extent, architects, engineers.

"I hope this general disbelief will gradually be dispelled as more and more people begin to accept the idea of the existence of elemental beings who are prepared to help man, and so hasten the cooperation with their kingdom. I can visualise new kinds of horticulture and agriculture being developed as well as harmful methods being discarded.

"It cannot be emphasised enough that the elemental beings and their god, Pan, are servants of God and function according to His will only." [60]

Roc believed that in certain times in the past such contact was possible and even easy. No doubt, he reasoned, that man had to lose his sensitivity and awareness in order to develop his intellect. The time has now come when the sensitivity is gradually being renewed, a time of balance. Man will retain his intellect while heightening his awareness of other dimensions of reality.

I continue to come across usually young Irish adults who are involved in the ecological movements who would not necessarily be classified as country folk. Unlike some of their contemporaries they do not hold the faery-faith in contempt but have modernised it. The faeries retain their personalities, but their functions have become better understood, and there is less fear attached to them.

Early in my journeying to Ireland I had met an articulate woman named Sue who works creatively with the faery energy. Much of what she said was new to me at that time. Sue lives in a charming bridge house in the town of Clonegal, and immediately invited me in, delighted to share her knowledge and first-hand experience. Her organisation is also very active in the Irish ecological movement:

"We work with the faery, we recognise they are part of the spirit of the land. It is the faery that has been responsible for inspiring the Green Peace movement, as example.

"The first thing I had to learn about the faeries is that their vibration is different from ours, like a bee. It seems OK to the bee, but quite fast for us. They live in a different world, which parallels ours but doesn't coincide. They can slow themselves down and let us see them at a different speed. They slow down for us.

"I didn't know much about it until I came to Ireland. Everyone starts out with the media idea - they don't appear as you expect. I went for a walk in the forestry wandering along the trail. A strange bluish sort of object moved through the trees, but then as soon as I looked at it, it slowed down even more so I could see it and then it disappeared. It looked like a pigeon. You know how your mind tries to make sense out of what you see?"

I was to know precisely what she meant, but it was almost two years before I had a similar experience. As we relaxed over tea and cakes, she elaborated further:

"We also have house faeries, and they can be seen mostly in the autumn or winter. You can be sitting in a chair and suddenly across the way you see a grey darkish flitter out of the corner of your eye - no shape you can put to them. You think that you are going to get used to it, but it is always a surprise when you see them. Next time I will see more, for I felt I had been accepted. Once you are accepted, then you are always accepted. I am no longer amazed at the things they can do. Weird and strange and wonderful things.

"They are the naughty ones, they steal things and put them somewhere else. They stole a ring of mine around Oíche Shamhna, (Hallowe'en) which was missing off my finger. I thought it went into the pastry. No one found it. My youngest daughter found it under her bed in the fourth-story loft. No, no, I haven't been up there in her room for a long time, so I couldn't have lost it up there. They also steal tools and they turn up somewhere else."

Although she had only been in Ireland for a few years, she said:

"My first idea of faeries came after the second World War. My father worked in a munitions factory and he went to work on a bicycle. One day the bicycle received a puncture, and the bicycle pump that was usually next to the bicycle on the front porch was gone. Disappeared. So he had to walk, and when he got there the building had just blown up. The next day the pump was found in a place it was never put."

Sue's friend Charles explained that the nature spirits manifest in three general ways: in a form acceptable to the observer, hence the local variations; in a form that they wish to to convey a message; and in their pure energy form, seen mainly as a light phenomenon of some sort. He said that at one time a faery being appeared to him for a second as a "well-known Irish boxer" - the purpose being to convey to him the idea of strength and courage. These were traits he needed at that time of a crisis in his life.

I attended a workshop, with several local friends, at Meitheal. It was an eclectic retreat centre in Donegal, and had a fraternal connection with the Findhorn community in Scotland. Sitting on the very northern tip of the island of Inch, it was a centre for new-age speakers and events, most activities have a definite Irish identity. It was formed in part some years back by the energy of my friend Patricia, an attractive reed-thin woman from New Zealand.

Originally Meitheal was considered to be intrusive by the island residents, but limping efforts had been made on both sides to understand each other. This was implemented by the number of younger Irish Catholics who participated in the community and spoke well of it.

However, this particular workshop leader hailed from Los Angeles, California. Ashleah by name, she had been recommended by someone who did not know the community.

"I'm acutely uncomfortable with her," Patricia said, after listening to her morning presentation. "What will the locals think?"

"Well, Patricia," I said, "she is from California. She is not so strange there. But don't you tell anyone I'm from the same place she is."

"I think I need to meditate," was her reply.

Ashleah had expounded all morning to the thirty or so workshop attendees about how she had "personally" been "lifted into the space-ship of the Ashtar Command and returned to this planet with a new identity as the goddess Ashleah."

While there, she had been taken on a tour of the many chambers in the vessel. She described them at length, and told of the disincarnates she had met while so journeying. Although her flowing purple robe which attempted to cover her ample frame with grace caught some of the colours of the heather, and her hair was the colour of the bleached wheat of the fields, she was decidedly not a Celtic Goddess, nor was her voyage an Irish one.

Despite this, her audience cared for her, because they sensed that she had a heart for matters spiritual, and this they could identify with. Further, no matter how

outlandish her adventures were, they could match them. Being abducted by an alien was not a surprising thing to happen. But not by a space brother, rather a faery.

Patricia introduced me to Jane, whom I could safely guess had some ties to the elemental worlds. With her red hair and green eyes; her square, grounded shape; her reputation as a fortune teller, her knowledge of herbal cures - she surely could be one of "them".

She caught my eye, nodding toward Ashleah. "The emperor's new clothes, I'd say," she said, with a highly detectable devilment in her gaze.

"I'd say you were right", was my reply, conveying all that was necessary.

A young man who had earlier whispered to me in the meeting room, "I think it is all crap," was now intently talking about the elfin influence on Irish music. His thick brogue made some words unclear to even the most stalwart of listeners, but it didn't matter. It wasn't crap.

A lively young hairdresser from Derry, who with her crystals and ethnic clothes was not unlike a young woman in a California community said, "I used to see them when I was young. At least I think I did. At my parent's place. They said I 'used to run with the faeries'. Now I sense them, I sense them all the time. I think they help me with my creative work."

There was more talk of the faery and of the myths. After a time I briefly told them what I was doing, but my assignment was so acceptable that it didn't even cause a ripple in the conversation. It was utterly natural, utterly coherent, utterly sensible. Utterly Irish. I had lost my identity as a Californian and was absorbed by the culture I had come to study.

I had first met Mark at the week-long Earthcamp Seminar in County Roscommon in August of 1993. Mark is also no stranger to the faery energy, although he is not of Irish heritage, but Jewish. A group of about 50 of us were there to discuss matters of environmental concern and interest.

Mark had come to the camp "intuitively" after he had seen an advertisement for the camp, and we were not only the only "fresh" Americans there, but also the only two staying at an obscure B&B fairly far removed from the lecture hall. Since I had my Diahatsu KK and he had no transportation, I chauffeured him around, and we found we had many common ties in the consciousness movement in the States.

As well as visiting the Celtic lands in general, he was going to stay with a woman friend of his. She was a therapist enrolled in a Jungian graduate program in Dublin. "Marita is her name. You would like her, Kay."

Mark visited me in Donegal at the end of his stay in the Celtic lands, a few weeks after the camp. His opening remark was, "Guess what. Marita knows you. You two have corresponded, and she still has a letter of yours."

It was then it clicked. She was one of the faery people in our small network of less than 20 people. I had lost contact with her completely, as her last known address was in Phoenix, Arizona, USA. I indeed did re-unite with her, to the delight of us both. She is another of the faery demeanour, barely five feet tall.

A mutual friend said of her, "I'm not sure she is always so tangible. I looked at her once...we were walking in the woods. She looked as if she might blend right into a tree."

For many years Mark had been the right hand man for the Maharishi Mahesh Yoga, the guru of the transcendental meditation movement. Not only was he a messenger for Marita and me, but he is very knowledgeable about the different states of perceptual higher awareness which his spiritual practices had help him to experience. This is his story of a faery encounter he had some years back. His sighting shows that the little people not only inhabit other lands, but don the national costumes as well!

"We had this quiet, long time in Switzerland, particularly around the Hotel Hertenstein on Lake Lucerne. It was a beautiful, idyllic area. I had some time to myself, and could take long walks. I had just finished doing some longer meditations, and was in a fairly clear state at the time.

"On these walks I would often have very, very clear perceptions of the little people. I saw around fifteen to twenty different little entities. They were between three and four feet tall on the average, and were actually very civilised looking.

"They had on their outfits. Most of them that I saw were male. The females were more illusive and less distinct and clear to me than the males were. Often they had on earth colours - browns and greens. In four or five cases, they actually stopped and looked at me and I would look at them. We would kind of assess each other. They were clearly not real people. They weren't anywhere near that solid.

162

"I actually got about three feet from one of them. Our paths crossed, and I didn't really become aware of him until we were quite close. He looked like a little Burgermeister with a round belly, and had on a brown suit with a vest, a hat, and shoes. He had long stockings on, and his pants didn't go all the way to his ankles - knickerbockers I believe they are called.

"He was the most solid one that I saw and he was almost like a little man, but I obviously knew that if I tried to pass my hand through him it would go right through.

"I don't know how to describe this, but I had a sense that he was there and not there at the same time. If he were a man, I wouldn't have that sense at all. Not a human being, he wasn't as clearly of this dimension - or this solid reality - as a person is. I knew he could disappear at any moment, as some of them did.

"In this case, we assessed each other for at least a minute, and during this time he was most visible. As we started walking in opposite directions, he became more transparent. Then I looked back, and I couldn't see anything at all. He was gone from my ability to perceive him, or he chose to disappear, whatever."

Not to be outdone by these etheric athletes, I finally saw something out of the corner of my eye. It was not cloven-hoofed like Kurmos, nor was it John's wee woman or Mark's properly dressed Burgermeister, not even Sue's rolled-up Pigeon. It was peculiar to me.

It was a warm and forgiving Sunday in Donegal, and although as a local said the sun wasn't "fond of visitin' these parts this year," it did occasionally grace us that day. If one is wise in this country, "you go out with yourself" when the weather invites.

A hike was in order. I was looking for an illusive lake which was adjacent to the forest preserve, but it was not on an access road, and even the locals had trouble locating it. It was mid-afternoon, and my friend Mark and I were walking at a natural pace in the forest preserve.

While walking through a dense part of the woods I saw an incredible, inexplicable sight out of the corner of my eye. Just for a mere second, no more. I froze in my steps and looked again, but it had vanished completely.

What caught my eye was a large iridescent object seeming to be in movement through the forest canopy. Opaque in appearance and oval in shape, it was an intense blue in colour, almost royal blue, and was surrounded by a golden,

163

shining rim. About three or four feet in diameter, it appeared at eye level about thirty feet from me. If I were to try to describe what object it could be compared to, I would be at a loss for words. I would almost have to paint it to picture it accurately. It simply didn't look like anything I had seen before.

There was no noise, no bird, nor bright sun. No explanation. What was it? Migraine? Hit by a branch? I didn't even have a slight headache, the nearest tree was well away. It could not have been caused by looking at the sun as it was cloudy when last I glanced up.

Surprised and somewhat embarrassed, I asked Mark if he had seen it. He had not, but when I hesitantly told him what I had seen, he immediately suggested that it could have been the "energy form of a nature spirit".

As they say here, I am between two minds on the experience. Yet I need to remind myself that on that perfect day I found the lake. Without a mistake. It was only when I was on top of the mountain looking down at the forest that I realised out of a myriad of possibilities, it was the only accessible trail to the lake.

A moment of encouragement, of divine humour, to let us all know that we can be guided by inspiration when we allow it. What if I had actually seen an angel out of the corner of my eye?

Mark, who has learned much of the ways of meditation, helped me integrate this experience, reiterating the words of Spirit. He explained that from time to time, given particular circumstances, certain individuals are able to perceive many dimensions, including that of the faery. The following description is of an encounter he had in Ireland, and was told to me after I had met my Visitor. This particular sighting may have been dismissed by someone less trained in recognising the range of possibilities:

"I was walking near Lough Gara in County Roscommon on this small dirt road. I became aware that there was some kind of presence about two hundred yards away in between two trees, where the wind was blowing. I saw an energy configuration, where there was more energy than everywhere else, and the energy was taking form and was pulsating and radiating energy from a central form, a small ball of concentrated energy. The form was fairly diffuse: it was almost like a point or a small ball. It seemed to be a body in its own right. I could see an aura around this ball. It was almost as if it were a generator, but it was clearly a presence - some kind of conscious, embodied being.

"I internally greeted it for probably a couple of minutes. This globe of energy seemed to grow in intensity as we communed in this limited way, and then it de-intensified as that period passed. Then it clearly wasn't there anymore.

"At times I have seen things like that much more clearly, where they actually have a human like form, but are also clearly changeable in their shape and illusive. You will see them for a few seconds, or a split second, and then they are gone."

XVIII

Fesba of the Faeries

I returned to California for the winter of 1993, and did not return to Ireland until early spring of 1994. It was a long and welcome visit. My family was less apprehensive of my project than in previous times, as I had a credible manuscript in hand, complete with positive comments from my editors and some of the exquisite works of my illustrator. Later I would receive the gift of the lyrical poetry found throughout the book, given by the very well-recognised and accomplished poet and native Irish speaker, Gabriel Rosenstock.[12] My youngest daughter Lynn commented, "Mother, even a normal person could read this."

My middle daughter's husband calls me "the great white leprechaun hunter". Both asked me to bring home a live faery to pre-school Sammy as a trophy. My eldest daughter, Shelly, encouraged me to continue my role as an "itinerant author" as "you will really be too old some day".

Her daughter, Christine, whom Spirit initially identified as one of the faery clan, was then four years of age. Although she talks of faeries and angels consistently, whether she actually "sees" them in her urban environment I could only conjecture.

While I was cleaning out my files in the States I came across this strange and oddly prophetic "poem" I wrote for some graduate class in the study of the Jungian intuitive function, way back probably in 1977. What I remember of the assignment was that we were to go into a deep meditation, and then record what came out of it, not censoring, not judging.

I was ashamed of it at the time and never finished it, or submitted it. Nothing came of it, but it must have touched me somehow because I kept it. This is it:

Nightsong

I am Nightsong, Birdwing, Daughter of Reflection
I am born again only in the darkness of night,
When the moon shines upon the still mountain lake

I am gossamer-winged, the evening rainbow
My wings are of pure blue, of deep violet as the spring flower,
of pink as the budding of the wild rose

My garments woven from threads of myriads of spider webs,
my hair the hue of the earth's bower

I was born in the time of eternal darkness,
when only silence was above the sphere

The land was filled with music,
without pain, without sin

Each spring I shall return again as the white lily
and I will find the Spirit within...

Essentially it is a poem about a faery transmigrate who came here to be of assistance. There are so many themes in the poem that are apt. The name-changing, the spirit entity, not being earth bound, the helping function. Almost a synopsis of what Spirit would tell me well over a decade later.

On my return to Ireland this time I stayed for a few days with my friend Jim in Belfast. As he picked me up at the airport, he said, "While you were gone, there was a man who was interviewed on the local talk show. He was talking about a family who had a little faery man living with them."

"So, tell me more," I said, knowing for sure I was back in Ireland. "I've heard of them eating dinner with people and then disappearing and the like, or coming on many different occasions to see a particular person. But not living over such a long period. Here we go again, another part of the mystery."

Jim said, "A man from Ballymoney was on the Seán Rafferty radio program. He had just published a book on folklore. It seems a friend of his in his youth had come upon a family who was caretaking a little faery man. Oh, it was a true story, it was.

"There used to be all kinds of those men around, living in the Glens of Antrim, the ones who met up with the faery people. They'd be all alone by themselves, talking to no one but their sheep and their dogs. They are dying out now, but there used to be a lot of them.

"There were other people who had faery residents as part of the family. They were looked at as their own children. There is a lot of girls who became pregnant and it was blamed on the faeries.

"You can disbelieve about the faeries here in Ireland, but it won't do you much good. Now, it is easy to do it in New York or California, but it's not easy to do it here in Ireland."

Jim went on to tell me a joke about the differences in perceptions of the Americans and the Irish, a subject that both of us were considerably more sophisticated about than we were a year ago when we first met. Character-istically, he was talking about sex, one of his favourite subjects.

"There were some American troops stationed in the Ballymoney area in 1943. They had plenty of girl friends, but on friendly relationship only. Eventually one of them became so frustrated he asked a local girl, straight forward:

"What do girls do about sex in Ballymoney?"

"Sergeant, most girls here have their evening tea about sex o'clock. That's why you don't see any girls around that time," was her quick reply.

I first met Jim in 1991 in Carmel after my first Irish odyssey. He was the father of a young friend of my mother, and was on one of his periodic visits to her from Ireland.

"Would you like to meet him?" my mother said. "He is known to be a good storyteller. You might remember, he stayed with me some years back when I was renting a room, just before you moved in after your separation. I found him to be of good character and intelligent."

I was subsequently introduced to Jim at a gathering in Carmel, but had no time then to collect stories and I thought no more of the meeting. At the time, however, I was somewhat on the lookout for an Irishman not too much taller than I. Spirit had mentioned during initial conversations quite a while back that I would meet a very gentle and loving man while on this quest that I could have a long term relationship with if I wished - not surprisingly, someone very Irish.

I took Spirit's announcement as a cosmic bribe, but a welcome one. I hadn't considered Jim as a possible contender for the mystery man for several reasons. I thought he was very married (eight children), that he was Scottish in background, and because he was a businessman from Belfast he would not be the least interested in matters of spirit. Further, from my mother's description of him, he didn't sound too interesting.

Yet, in the early fall of 1992, my mother wrote to me and suggested I get in touch with Jim again. "His daughter thinks he will be a good contact for you, and will probably come and visit you as he is fond of Donegal. He is recently divorced, and is enrolled in college for the first time and intends to graduate." Divorce, grown children, a career change. Like me, the full catastrophe.

I followed her suggestion, and Jim and I began corresponding. I was about to return to California late that fall when I had an unexpected free weekend, and asked him over as my mother had suggested. Never have I been entertained so abundantly. Flowers, chocolates, my refrigerator filled with food, a good bottle of brandy. Not much above my head, he looks a bit like a leprechaun ready to play a joke.

170

Although lithe and thin for his seventy some years, he is not fond of unnecessary exercise. "It is good to lie down to relax the muscles that have gotten stressed from sitting," he explained.

And Juno. Juno is his shy, sweet but extremely determined female Doberman who goes everywhere with him. This includes a daily run, with Jim following her in his Honda while she runs alongside the road. An amusing spectacle for the locals, who were definitely taking note of the entire situation.

He talked a lot about Ireland that weekend, as he did every subsequent weekend he visited. The history of it, of the men and women of Ireland, of the church, of the oppression, of the repression of sexuality. What I might do to make the faeries a little more interesting. "You need to put a little randy in their step. You know, like describing some amazing appendages!"

Jim understands quite well my interest in the faeries, but does not think me crazy because of that. Although he will not always admit it, he also believes in the little ones. The idea of "descending from the faeries" is not a foreign concept to him either.

"There were young girls who lived in remote areas in the mountains of Mourne who were considered to be from the faeries. They were delicate looking usually, not like the strong farmer girls. Often they didn't live beyond their early years. Wouldn't do too well between two buckets."

Yet, he has confided to me on several occasions that anyone coming from California to live in windy and blustery Donegal must be more than daft, demented, most likely. In this way he questions my deviation from normality, not because of my lineage. Like many Irish, he has little interest in the new-age phenomena in the manner it is being presented in the States.

When Jim took me to the Ulster Folk Museum in Belfast I walked into a simulated room that was grandmother Mullin's parlour. The same type furniture, colours, style. In the sewing section were the same handiwork, and quilt designs of grandmother Sprague. She was a seamstress of Ulster background, as was his mother.

Is he this compatible one? Who knows. He is obtaining his college degree he was deprived of in his youth. I admire him for doing this at 70, but he is moving away from a mystery that I am moving towards. It won't do any harm to wait a bit and see. It is another good reason to be in Ireland for a while.

I traced the story Jim heard on the radio about the faery man. It was a true story of the wee man who came out of the faery fort. So well told in a just published local account, the "wee man" had red hair and a red beard that hung down over his knees. He was about two feet six inches tall, and was "the smallest man I ever saw," according to the story teller.

The wee man purportedly lived with a family in the Ballymoney district, and when the family moved there was no further trace of the unusual house guest. The observer only saw him twice, but others in the neighbourhood had also seen him and were quite aware of his presence. The red-haired guest apparently came to his adopted family one wild night and stayed an indefinite period of time. Unfortunately, the story is fragmented, as it all happened nearly a century ago.

"But it did happen. It was my friend who told me it, and it was his father-in-law who saw him, and I believe them. There was no cause to lie about it," the author stated.[61]

It seems a bit too much, even for Ireland. But so do the moving rocks, the peculiar birds, the ghost ships, and the lot.

I found this tale during my research in a small book called *Legendary Stories of The Carlingford Lough District*. First published in 1913, it had long since been unavailable until it was reprinted recently. Other charming stories include the *Long Woman's Grave*, *The Vampire Tree*, and *King of the Rath*. None as poignant as the following, however. Entitled the *Quatre-Foil Gift Voice*, simplified in part it reads:

> *I'll seek a Four-Leaved Shamrock*
> *In all the faery dells,*
> *And if I find the charmed leaf*
> *Oh, how I'll weave my spells.*

"The lucky finder of the plant of the Gaelic Gods, the Four-Leaved Shamrock, has choice of four gifts - the Wisdom of Lugh; the Power of the Dagda; the Love-Gift of Angus Óg; or the gift of the Song of Dana - the invocation of the Faery Muse.

"One beautiful spring morning there was a christening in the cottage by the Fort of Lisnagushee (Fort of the Faery-Voice), high on Aughnamoira Hill. Before bringing the infant-girl Fesba to the church to be christened, her godparent, a young colleen, stole out to the green fort and returned with a Four-Leaved Shamrock, its magic petals still wet and glistening with the faery dew. She

172

quickly placed it under the infant's tongue and wished for the invocation of the Faery Muse so that Fesba might be the Child of Song.

"As she so wished a sudden change came over the room. There was a faint eerie sound, and a misty vapour filled the atmosphere. The Faery Muse appeared by the colleen's side, and laid a tender hand on the infant's head. "Have thou the gift of Song," she said.

"She poured 'faery-mel' in Fesba's mouth that her voice might be sweet; and with a sounding sea-shell, blew a song in her ears for melody. Placing her hand on the child's forehead she then bathed her eyes with lusmore juice (herbal extract, foxglove plant) so that they were opened to the sights of the *sidhe*.

"The muse then touched her throat, and the Shamrock became indelibly imprinted on her throat as a sign of the Gift-Voice that was to be hers. It was also the symbol of the Muse, who marked her for her own:

I take thy heart as I touch thy hand,
I bind thee with a mystic band;
And give thee power to understand,
As the soul of a star be the soul in thee.
From the world's dark mists secure and free,
In the shadow of earth burning radiantly.
Thou shalt bathe in the moon's pale light,
Under the secret curtains of night,
And know and drink of its cool delight.
Down in the glades where the tall lusmore
Grows 'neath the oak-trees branches hoar,
By the streams where the faery cataracts pour,
Thou shalt follow me, thou shalt go,
The silver shining lakes below,
And know the joys the mystic know.

"The Muse then faded away. The manifestation lasted only a few minutes, but to the scared colleen it seemed an age. She confessed the ceremony to the parents. All did what they could to remove the Voice-Mark, but to no avail. They then consulted a faery doctor, who gave them a counter-charm of magical herbs for protection of the infant.

"Nevertheless, one night of the full moon the Muse came to collect her ward - a silvery vision in misty flowing raiment, gliding softly round the end of the house, clasping the child in her arms. Three times she knocked to give warning, and if she chanced to meet a mortal before she reached the fort, she would be obliged to offer the babe back. The father awoke and intercepted, and brought Fesba back to safety.

"On constant vigilance after this, there was not an inch of her garments but something sacred was sewed there to ward off the mystic power. The parents lived under a vague indefinite shadow, which was more fearsome than mortal danger; it was intangible, but it was still real and always there. They felt they were attended by an unseen being. If the babe smiled in her sleep, the Muse was whispering in her ear. The mother held her in a close embrace, knowing their efforts to keep her must prove hopeless.

"The years rolled by and Fesba had grown up a beautiful colleen, but slight and ethereal, with a dreamy spiritualised face. Her fathomless blue eyes had the far-away look of *Tír na nÓg* in their depths, foretelling a short earthly span.

"Reared on the lonesome hill, surrounded by mounts, forts, and dullow bushes, and living in an atmosphere of traditions and beliefs, her mind was fed on the folklore that floated over the border from the spirit-world. Hearing herself spoken of as the Spell-Child of the Faery Muse, it took possession of her sense to such an extent that she considered herself of the spirit-world and not of earth.

"She could see the spirits everywhere, faces in flowers and souls in plants. The very earth felt different to her, and the voice of the *sidhe* always sounded in her ears like the murmur of the sea-shell, calling her far from earth to follow shadows.

"In the summer evenings she would sit for hours under the faery thorn, lulled into a bewitched sleep by the slumber-music of the silvery bell-branches. In the silence of the night she would arise in a trance-like sleep and leave the house to circle the Fort-ring, looking at scenes invisible to mortal eyes.

"Though the magic sights were everywhere to her, the old fort was her favourite place, and try how they would to keep her from it, there they still would find her - an elfin like figure, looking more like one of the *sidhe* than a creature of flesh and blood.

"She was the Spirit of Song incarnate, every breath was a note of music breathed out in harmony, the Spirit of Music had entered her being. She was always singing in joy or sorrow, and could no more keep silent than the wild birds of spring-time. She made known all her feelings in song. With such enthusiasm did she sing, and with such delight did she fill the hearts of the hearers that her fame spread far and wide, and all marvelled at the Gift-Singer.

"The people of her native place rejoiced more in the sound of her magic voice than they did in the songs of the birds; they listened as she roamed the hills singing, and the Gift-Voice came to their ears like the voice of Niamh, the spirit-maid from the Magic Isles.

"Alas, a wasting illness took hold of Fesba in her eighteenth year, causing her to become more frail and shadowy - 'faery-struck' folks called it. She had squandered her life in song, but wearied of mortals' praise.

"At this time a shepherd youth heard her sing, and ever after he could hear nothing but her voice, and see nothing but the maiden of the spell, and often he would leave his charge, and wander forth to hear the inspired of the Muse.

"At first she welcomed him, but feeling he would prevail on her to abandon the goal of her thoughts, she felt in despair; she knew her wasting illness would soon bring her short life to a close. It was fading fast, how fast she felt keenly, she was worried by the war of body and spirit, and to linger was to fail.

"'Why do you stray by the fearsome lochs, and frequent the haunted raths and springs; and give up earthly joys and love to follow shadows?' asked the shepherd youth.

"'I am never alone; I commune with friends always. I am not of this world, my gaze is fixed beyond the earth,' was her reply.

"He implored her to abandon the quest of the unattainable, and not to sacrifice human affection for a dream - the shadow for the reality.

"'The mortal life is unreal to me, the dream-life is reality,' she insisted:

> We who have walked in wonder-lands,
> Where Finn and Oscar rest;
> Who ride white-steeds with Manannan,
> At sunset down the West;
> We who have seen the Dagda's host

In glory rise again,
What reck we in a plodding land,
The little days of men...

"The heavenly faery music now sounded in Fesba's ears, wooing her away from love and earth, and she followed to the Fort. The witchery of the *sidhe* was round Fesba. The low voice of the Muse said, 'Now is the moment, cast the counter-charm from you and you are free.' She flung it from her and saw the Muse before her, with outstretched hands, saying, 'I come.' She fell forward on the Fort-ring in seeming death.

"The loss of Fesba was too much for her bereaved parents, and they both laid down and never rose again. Often above the Fort a voice is heard singing in the air, and it is the voice of Fesba of the Four-Leaved Shamrock, pouring out her captive soul in song forever." (62)

Is this then, a fairy tale, or is it the real tale of a faery? It is classified as a legend, yet legends often know more of truth than we have in this closed-off world. Does it rest on "primitive beliefs" as the careful collector insisted? Rather, it is quite sophisticated.

I salute you, Fesba of the Faeries. I honour the Preservers of your Tale. Blithe Spirit are you, Holders of the True Tradition are they.

Fesba's insistence that the otherworld is the real world echoes the truths in all the great spiritual teachings. This is the world of maya, illusion. Fesba lived in the time when there was correspondence between the dimensions. She was able to crossover, to penetrate the veil, and to her it did not mean annihilation. My dedication to the project is now complete. The doubts I had in the beginning have been wafted away by a consistently good humoured adventure.

The Road to Donegal has hardly come to a dead end. Perhaps, instead, it has become a little smoother because it has nearly left the ground! I feel I am often walking on air with delight because of what I have found here.

Ireland has witnessed so very much hardship, violence and oppression, and yet has always been a land of great spiritual strength. It is the land of renewal, and many will come here to experience purification of the heart. Its people shall become spiritual leaders of the world. That has always been their destiny.

Mac Cana points to this truth when he states that "in a tradition where the natural and the supernatural realms frequently converge it is not surprising that there is a constant awareness of the relativity of time and space...the land of Ireland itself, with its place-names and physical features, seems to shift with enigmatic ease between the two levels of perception...the contrasting effects of changing perspective as when the god Manannan describes the sea as a flowery plain or the monks of Clonmacnois observe a boat sailing in the sky over their head and drop its anchor by their church door..." [63]

Why the faery is seen, heard and sensed here more often than anywhere else in the world is still mysterious. The whole of it has been attributed to the Celtic imagination, and yet no mention is made of why the Irish-American immigrant does not often claim to see faeries in the forests or fields outside of Boston or even in the Ozarks, while his brother or sister still sees them dancing in Donegal.

I am just beginning to understand the secret a little. Life is simpler, more contemplative. Many rural Irish live in a state of meditation naturally. It is a good place to listen to God. Peace within is very important. The nature spirits will not come to one until there is peace of mind and peace of heart.

Ireland is a land where "the quiet reality of the faeries is still accepted as a matter of everyday truth, a normal part of life". The world has long made jest of what the rural seer has been seeing and sensing all along, but the derision hasn't obliterated the reality. He or she is attuned rather than out of tune, a new age expert rather than out of date. His or her head may be in the stars, but with feet solidly on holy ground.

The faery has always been a "good neighbour" in this land. Just because something doesn't happen very often doesn't mean it doesn't happen at all. One of the Gateways to Faery is here in this land, and some day the gates will swing wide open. Proof has been given me of the presence of the little people. The faery, the good people, those of the hill and sea have been continuously sighted, heard, felt and sensed since the beginning. They await our awakening and continue to inspire, amuse, and perplex us, causing havoc with the emotions and shaking the rational mind out of its complacency.

Spirit has told us that we have been asleep in the middle of heaven, and that the separation has amounted to half a blink. Enough of darkness, I surely think. Let's open our eyes and finish the blink. And look out of the corner of our eyes when we do, and see the beginning of the Grand Adventure.

178

Let us show you
herbs and leaves and bark
after dark

Let us show you
Root and stem -
more precious than a gem

Into this world of tortured feeling
All we bring is the gift of healing

We are the many and we are the few
We are the glistening morning dew

Let us show you
all you desire -
Water, air, earth and fire!

Footnotes

1 Called after Colm Cille ("Dove of the Church"), poet, holy man, druid. A fellow monk peeped in one night and Colm Cille was busy on a manuscript, one hand held aloft as bright as a candelabra.

2 *Imram* occurs in many tales of sea voyages, esoterically voyages of the spirit: *Imram Brain maic Febail, Imram Curaig Miledin, Imram Snedgusa ocus Maic Riagla*, etc. Unfortunately, Gaelic literature is not as widely edited, published and translated, and still remains in the scholastic rather than the public domain.

3 In local usage this word means not only the landed gentry, but also refers, in a fearfully respectful sense, to the faeries. "We call them the gentry, we do, so as not to offend them, you see," is not an uncommon local remark.

4 *braon ailse* - the corrosive drop, its impact measured in eons.

5 It is usually called Irish, to distinguish it from its near relations, Scots-Gaelic and Manx Gaelic. Irish belongs to the Indo-European language group and is a Celtic tongue. Celtic tongues fall into two main groups, one group changing the qu sound into p (ancient Gaulish, Welsh, Breton and Cornish). The second group represents the qu sound as c, Irish and its descendants, Scots-Gaelic and Manx. It has about 20,000 native speakers. Between 80 and 100 books are published yearly in Irish.

6 The White Mare and the White Cow are Gaelic metaphors for the Milky Way.

7 The Annals were composed chiefly by the Ó Clerys, hereditary historians to the Ó Donnells, Princes of Tyrconnel, now the County of Donegal. The work was begun in 1632, and transcribed in the convent of the Brothers of Donegal. Father Bernardine Ó Clery, born in 1580, was the chief author.

8 The primary meaning of *sidh* is a mound where dwelt the hill people, an aboriginal tribe who occasionally abducted a child of the settled tribe, thus giving rise in part to the myth of the *siofra* or changeling. Up to recent times, boys were dressed as girls to deceive the marauding faeries. Some adepts claim that *sidh* is linguistically cognate with *sidha*, one endowed with supernatural powers, just as the Boyne is related, linguistically, with Govinda (Krishna), "Fair Cow".

9 Faery pack of hounds.

10 The *Badhbh* (pronounced to rhyme with hive) is another appelation of the banshee. In ancient Ireland she was the war-goddess, appearing in the form of a scald-crow or *préachán ingneach* - crow with the fierce claws - foretelling slaughter and rejoicing over the slain.

11 The term *bean feasa* translated means a wise woman or woman of knowledge, a mediator, a seer. The *bean feasa* was a type of go-between of the supernatural, the faery world on the one hand and the ecclesiastical world on the other, establishing a sort of spiritual equilibrium in the community. One of her functions was to counteract the result of spells cast by evil-wishers, and of faery mischief.

12 Minette Quick, mentioned in an early chapter, was inspired by Gabriel Rosenstock's poetry which is found throughout this book. She set the poems to music and Gabriel agreed to speak the poetry himself. The result is The Fairy Thorn, Bringer of Light, and is available and described in catalogue form through North Star Music, P O Box 868, Cambridge, CB1 6SJ, UK.

Bibliography

Andrews, Elizabeth F.R.A.T. *Ulster Folklore*, Elliott Stock, London, 1913.

Annals of Clonmacnoise Being Annals of Ireland From The Earliest Period To AD. 1408, The, Translated into English in 1627, and edited by the Re. Denis Murphy, S. J., University Press for the Royal Society of Antiquaries of Ireland, 1896.

Annals of The Kingdom of Ireland By The Four Masters, Vol. 1, Edited by John O' Donovan, L .L. D., M.R. I. A., Hodges, Smith and Co., Dublin, 1856.

Arguelles, Jose. A. *Earth Ascending*, Shambala, Boulder and London, 1984.

Arrowsmith, Nancy with Moorse, George. *A Field Guide to the Little People*, Pocket Books, Simon and Schuster, NY, NY, 1977.

Aurobindo, Sri. *The Future Poetry*, Sri Aurobindo Ashram, Pondicherry, India, 1953.

Aurobindo, Sri. *The Life Divine*, Sri Aurobindo Ashram, Pondicherry, India, 1960.

Bailey, Alice. *A Treatise on Cosmic Fire*, Lucas Publishing Co., NY, NY, 1977.

Bailey, Alice. *Letters on Occult Meditation*, Lucas Publishing Co., NY, NY, 1979.

Bamford, Christopher with Marsh, William Parker. *An Anthology: Celtic Christianity Ecology and Holiness*, Lindisfarne Press, Hudson, NY, USA, 1987.

Bardon, Patrick. *The Dead Watchers and Other Folk-lore Tales of Westmeath*, Westmeath Guardian, Mullingar, Co. Westmeath, Ireland, 1891.

Barker, Cicely Mary. *A Flower Fairies Postcard Book*, Penguin, London, 1991.

Berry, James. *Tales of the West of Ireland*, The Dolman Press, Dublin, 1966.

Besant, Annie. *A Study in Consciousness*, Theosophical Publishing House, London, 1907.

Besant, Annie. *The Ancient Wisdom*, The Theosophical Press, Wheaton, Illinois, 1967.

Bett, Henry. *English Myths and Traditions*, B.T. Batsford, London, 1952.

Blair, Anna. *Scottish Tales*, Richard Drew Publishing Co., Glasgow, Scotland, 1987.

Blatavansky, H.P. *An Abridgment of the Secret Doctrine*, Facsimile of the original edition, The Theosophy Co., Los Angeles, CA., USA, 1974. 1st published by The Theosophical Publishing Co., Limited, NY, NY, 1888.

Bloom, William. *Devas Fairies and Angels*, Gothic Image Publications, Glastonbury, England, 1986.

Briggs, Katharine. *The Anatomy of Puck: An Examination of Fairy Beliefs Among Shakespeare's Contemporaries and Successors*, Routledge and Kegan Paul, London, 1959.

Briggs, Katharine. *The Vanishing People A Study of Traditional Fairy Beliefs*, B.T. Batsford Ltd. London, 1978.

Buntings Ancient Music of Ireland, edited from the original manuscripts by Donal O'Sullivan with Mícheál Ó Súilleabháin, Cork University Press, Cork, Ireland.

Burnham, Sophy. *A Book of Angels*, Ballantine Books, NY, NY, 1990.

Byrne, Patrick. *Witchcraft in Ireland*, Mercier Press, Cork, Ireland, 1967.

Caddy, Eileen. *The Spirit of Findhorn*, Harper and Rowe, San Francisco, CA, USA, 1976.

Carmichael, Alexander, Editor. *Carmina Gadelica, Vol. V.*, Oliver and Boyd, Edinburgh, Scotland, 1954.

Campbell, Patrick. *Rambles Round Donegal*, Mercier Press, Dublin, 1992. 1st. published 1981.

Carey, Ken. *Return of the Bird Tribes*, Harper Collins, NY, NY, 1988.

Carton, Hugh D. *True Stories Poetry and Folklore of Ireland*, Plantation Press, Lisburn, Co. Antrim, Northern Ireland, 1993.

Christiansen, Reidar Th. *Some Notes On The Fairies and the Fairy Faith*, in Béaloideas, The Journal of the Folklore of Ireland Society, University College Dublin, Dublin, Volume 39-41, 1971-1973.

Colum, Pádraic. *Legends of Hawaii*, Yale University Press, New Haven, Connecticut, USA, 1937.

Course in Miracles, A, Foundation for Inner Peace, Tiburon, CA., USA.

Cousin, James. *New Ways in English Literature*, Ganesh and Co., Madras, India, 1917.

Crawford, Michael G. *Legendary Stories of the Carlingford Lough District*, V.G. Havern, Warrenpoint, Northern Ireland, 1913. Re-issued, no date.

Croker, T. C. *Fairy Legends and Traditions of the South of Ireland*, John Murray, London, 1828.

Croker, T. C. *Legends of Kerry*, Geraldine Press, Tralee, Co. Kerry, Ireland, 1972.

Curtin, Jeremiah. *Irish Folk Tales*, The Educational Co. of Ireland, Dublin, 1943.

Curtin, Jeremiah. *Tales of the Fairies and of the Ghost World* Collected from Oral Tradition in South-West Munster, Lemma Publishing Corp. NY, NY, 1970.

Danaher, Kevin. *Folktales of the Irish Countryside*, Mercier Press, Cork, Ireland, 1967.

de Purucker, G. *The Esoteric Tradition*, Vol. 1, Theosophical University Press, Pasadena, USA, 1935.

Devas and Men, edited by Southern Center of Theosophy, Robe, South Australia,Theosophical Publishing House, Adyar Madrad, India, 1977.

Devereux, Paul. *Earth Lights Revelation*, Blandford Press, London, 1990.

Devereux, Paul. *Places of Power*, Artillery House, London, 1990.

Doyle, Arthur Conan. *The Coming of the Fairies*, The Psychic Press, London, 1928.

Evans-Wentz, W.Y. *The Fairy-Faith in Celtic Countries*, Oxford University Press, 1911, new edition with foreword by Kathleen Raine, Colin Smythe, Gerrards Cross, England, 1977.

Evans-Wentz, W. Y. *Tibet's Great Yogi Milarepa*, Oxford University Press, Oxford, England, 1969.

Findhorn Community, *The Findhorn Garden*, Harper and Rowe, NY, NY, 1975.

Fitzpatrick, Jim. *Erinsaga,* De Danann Press, Dublin, 1985.

Francis, Patrick. *The Grand Design - 111,* Amour Publications, Drogheda, Co. Louth, Ireland, 1993.

Funk and Wagnalls *Standard Dictionary of Folklore, Mythology and Legend,* edited by Maria Leach, New English Library, London, 1972.

Gantz, Jeffery. *Early Irish Myths and Sagas,* Penguin Books, London, 1981.

Gébler, Carlo, *The Cure,* Hamish Hamilton, Ltd., London, 1994.

Glassie, Henry. *Irish Folktales,* Pantheon Books, NY, NY, 1985.

Gregory, Lady Augusta. *Gods and Fighting Men,* Colin Smythe, Gerrards Cross, England, 1970. 1st published 1904.

Gregory, Lady Augusta. *Visions and Beliefs in the West of Ireland,* Colin Smythe, Gerrards Cross, 1970. 1st published 1920.

Haining, Peter. *The Leprechaun's Kingdom,* Granada Publishing Limited, London, 1981.

Hall, Manly. *Paracelsus. His Mystical and Medical Philosophy,* The Philosophical Research Society, Inc., Los Angeles, CA, USA, 1964.

Hall, Manly. *The Secret Teachings of All Ages,* The Philosophical Research Society, Inc., Los Angeles, CA, USA, 1964.

Hawken, Paul. *The Magic of Findhorn,* Harper and Rowe, NY, NY, 1975.

Hilarion. *Other Kingdoms,* Marcus Books, Queensville, Ontario, Canada, 1981.

Hodson, Geoffrey. *The Brotherhood of Angels and Men,* Theosophical Publishing House, Wheaton, Ill., USA, 1982.

Hodson, Geoffrey. *The Kingdom of Faerie,* Theosophical Publishing House, London, 1927.

Hope, Murray. *Practical Celtic Magic,* The Aquarian Press, Wellingborough, Northamptonshire, England, 1987.

Hyde, Douglas. *Beside the Fire - A Collection of Irish Gaelic Folk Stories,* David Nutt, London, 1890.

Hyde, Douglas. *Legends of Saints and Sinners,* Gresham, London, 1915.

Ingpen, Robert. *Australian Gnomes,* Rigby, Adelaide, Australia, 1979.

Ingpen, Robert with Page, Michael. *Encyclopedia of Things That Never Were,* Viking-Penguin, Inc. NY, NY, 1987.

Jarrett, Kinsley. *Visions of the Ascended Masters,* Spiral, Fitzroy, Australia, 1992.

Keating, Geoffrey, D. D. *The History of Ireland From The Earliest Period to the English Invasion,* Translated from the original Gaelic by John O' Mahony, James B. Kirker, New York, 1866.

Kirk, Robert. *The Secret Commonwealth of Elves, Fauns, and Faeries.* New edition in modern English with commentary by R. J. Stewart, published as Robert Kirk, Walker Between Worlds, Element Books, Shaftesbury, Dorset, England, 1990.

Larkin, David. Editor. *Faeries,* Peacock Press, Bantam, NY, NY, 1978.

Larmine, William. *West Irish Folk-Tales and Romances,* Elliott Stock, London, 1893.

Latham, Minor White. *The Elizabethan Fairies,* Colombia University Press, NY, NY, 1930.

Leahy, A.H. *Heroic Romances of Ireland*, Vol. 1, David Nutt, London, 1905.

Lenihan, Edmund. *In Search of Biddy Early*, Mercier Press, Dublin, 1987.

Logan, Patrick. *The Holy Wells of Ireland*, Colin Smythe, Gerrards Cross, England, 1980.

Logan, Patrick. *The Old Gods: The Facts About Irish Fairies*, Appletree Press, Belfast, Northern Ireland, 1981.

Lynch, Patricia. *Enchanted Irish Tales*, Mercier Press, Dublin, 1989.

Newhouse, Flower. *Natives of Eternity*, Lawrence Newhouse, Vista, CA, USA, 1950.

Mac Cana, Proinsias. *Celtic Mythology*, The Hamlyn Publishing Group Limited, Middlesex, England, 1968.

Mac Cana, Proinsias, Editor. *Celtic Religion*, in Encyclopedia of Religion, Miscea Eliade, Editor in Chief, Macmillan Publishing Co., NY, NY, 1987.

Mac Cana, Proinsias, Editor. *The Learned Tales of Medieval Ireland*, Dublin Institute for Advanced Studies, Dublin, 1980.

Mac Cana, Proinsias, Editor. *Literature in Irish*, Department of Foreign Affairs, Dublin, 1980.

Maclean, Dorothy. *To Hear the Angels Sing*, Lindisfarne Press, Hudson, NY, USA, 1990.

Mc Manus, Diarmuid. *Irish Earth Folk*, The Devin Adair Co., NY, NY, 1959.

MacRitchie, David. *Fians, Fairies and Picts*, Kegan Paul, Trench, Triibner and Co. Ltd, London, 1893.

MacRitchie, David. *The Testimony of Tradition*, Kegan Paul, Trench, Triibner and Co., Ltd., 1890.

Matthews, Caitlin. *The Elements of The Goddess*, Element Books, Shaftesbury, Dorset, England, 1989.

Matthews, Caitlin and John. *The Western Way: A Practical Guide to the Western Mystery Tradition, Vol. 1*, Arkana, London, 1986.

Meyer, Kuno *The Voyage of Bran - Son of Febal*, David Nutt, London, 1895.

Moray, Ann. *A Fair Stream of Silver*, Longmans, London, England, 1966.

Mythical and Fabulous Creatures, A Source Book and Research Guide, edited by Malcolm South, South Greenwood Press, Westport, Conneticut, 1987.

Ó Duilearga, Séamus. Editor. Seán Ó Conaill's Book: *Stories and Traditions from Iveragh*, University College Dublin, Dublin, 1981.

O Hanlon, Rev. John. *Irish Folk Lore: Traditions and Superstitions of the Country*, Cameron and Ferguson, Glasgow, Scotland, 1870.

Ó hÓgáin, Dáithi. *Myth, Legend and Romance of the Irish Folk Tradition*, Ryan Publishing Co., London, 1990.

Ó hEochaidh, Seán. *Fairy Legends From Donegal*, University College Dublin, Dublin, 1977.

O' Rahilly, Thomas. *Early Irish History and Mythology*, The Dublin Institute for Advanced Studies, Dublin, 1946.

O' Sullivan, Seán. *A Handbook of Irish Folklore*, Folklore Associates, Inc., Herbert Jenkins, London, 1963.

O' Sullivan, Seán. *Irish Folk Customs and Beliefs*, published for The Cultural Relations Committee of Ireland by Mercier Press, Cork, Ireland, 1967.

O' Sullivan, Seán. *Legends from Ireland*, B. T. Batsford Ltd., London, 1977.

Pierrakos, Eva. *The Pathwork of Self-Transformation*, Bantam Books, NY, NY, 1990.

Porteous, Alexander. *Forest Folklore, Mythology and Romance*, George Allen and Unwin, Ltd., London, 1928.

Readers Bible, The. London Oxford University Press, Cambridge University Press, Eyre and Spottiswoode, England, 1951.

Rees, Alwyn with Rees, Brinley. *Celtic Heritage*, Thames and Hudson, London, 1974.

Riddell, Carol. *The Findhorn Community*, Findhorn Press, Moray, Scotland, 1990.

Roads, Michael. *Journey into Nature*, H. J. Kramer, Inc., Tiburon, CA, 1990.

Robinson, Tim. *Stones of Aran Pilgrimage*, Penguin Books, London, 1990.

Rolleston, T.W. *Myths and Legends of the Celtic Race*, George G. Harrop and Co., London, 1919, later printed as Celtic, Studio Editions, London.

Russell, G. W. *The Descent of The Gods Comprising The Mystical Writings of G. W. Russell 'A.E.'*, edited by Raghavan Iyer with Nandin Iyer, Colin Smythe, Gerrards Cross, 1988.

Ryan, Meda. *Biddy Early: The Wise Woman of Clare*, Mercier Press, Ltd., Dublin, 1978.

Smith, Peter. *W. B. Yeats and the Tribes of Danu - Three views of Ireland's Fairies*, Colin Smythe, Gerrards Cross, England.

Spence, Lewis. *The Fairy Tradition in Britain*, Rider and Co., London, 1948.

Spence, Lewis. *The History and Origins of Druidism*, Samuel Weiser, NY, NY, 1971.

Squire, Charles. *Celtic Myth and Legend Poetry and Romance*, The Gresham Publishing Co., London, 1902.

Stephens, James. *The Crock of Gold*, Macmillan and Co., London, 1980. 1st published 1912.

Stewart, R. J. *Power Within The Land*, Element, Shaftesbury, Dorset, England, 1992, Element, Inc., Rockport, MA, USA, 1992.

Synge, J. M. *The Aran Islands*, Oxford University Press, Oxford, England, 1989. 1st published 1907.

Uí Ógáin, Ríonach. *Music Learned From the Fairies*, in Béaloideas, The Journal of the Folklore of Ireland Society, University College Dublin, Dublin, Vol. 60-1, 1992-1993.

Urantia Book, The. Urantia Foundation, Chicago, Ill., USA, 1955.

van Gelder, Dora. *The Real World of Fairies*, Theosophical Publishing House, London, 1977.

Westervelt, W. D. *Hawaiian Historical Legends*, Fleming H. Revell Co., London, 1923.

White, Carolyn. *A History of Irish Fairies*, Mercier Press, Dublin, 1976.

Wilde, Lady Jane. *Ancient Legends of Ireland*, Chatto and Windus, London, 1889.

Wilde, Lady Jane. *Irish Cures, Mystic Charms and Superstitions*, Sterling Publishing Co., Inc. NY, NY, 1991.

Wilde, Oscar. *The Poems and Fairy Tales of Oscar Wilde*, Modern Library, NY, NY, 1932.

Wright, Machaelle Small. *Behaving as if The God in All Life Mattered*, Perelandra, Jeffersonton, Virginia, 1987.

Wright, Machaelle. *The Perelandra Garden Workbooks 1 and 11*, Perelandra, Jeffersonton, Virginia, 1992.

Yeats, William Butler. *The Celtic Twilight,* Lawrence & Bullen, London, 1893. Still in print.

Yeats, William Butler. *Early Poems & Stories*, Macmillan & Co. Limited, London, 1925.

Periodicals:

Béaloideas, The Journal of the Folklore of Ireland Society, The Department of Irish Folklore, University College Dublin, Dublin, All issues. Vol. 1, 1928.

Music:

Carolyn's Receipt, A Collection of Carolyn's Music as Recorded (and arranged) by Derek Bell for Irish Harp, Neo Irish Harp and Tiompan, Lyra Music Co., NY, 1980.

Manx Music For The Irish Harp, arranged by Charles Guard, Charles Guard, Isle of Man, British Isles, 1991.

List of References:

1. Billie Ogden, who does psychic counselling can be contacted at Heartsong, P. O. Box 422, Sagle, Idaho, 83860. Psychic counsellor Paul Norman Tuttle also contributed. Called the Rajpur material, it is available through: Northwest Foundation For A Course In Miracles, P.O. Box 1490, Kingston, Washington. 98346.
2. Questhaven Retreat Center, A New Age Sanctuary and School of Christian Mysticism, 20506 Questhaven Road, Escondido, California, 92029.
3. Stephens, p. 228.
4. Glencolumbkille Heritage Center, Glencolumbkille, Co. Donegal, Ireland.
5. Jaya Alchemy Cards, The Source, 11 East Essex St, Dublin 2, Ireland.
6. Aurobindo, The Future Poetry, p. 252.
7. Bax, p. 103.
8. Russell. p. 562.
9. Mac Cana, Encyclopedia, p. 149.
10. Mac Cana, Literature, p. 12.
11. Evans-Wentz, Fairy-Faith, p. 3.
12. Briggs, The Vanishing People, pp. 7-8.
13. Keating, p. 139.
14. Annals of Clonmacnoise, p. 26.
15. Annals of the History of Ireland, p. 17.
16. Squire, p. 72.
17. Annals of the History of Ireland, p. 17.
18. Ibid, p. 24.
19. Annals of Clonmacnoise, p. 26.
20. Rees, p. 30.
21. Leahy, pp. 12-13.
22. Rees.
23. Rolleston, Myths, p. 136.
24. Mc Manus, p. 25.
25. Gregory, Visions and Beliefs, p. 71.
26. Campbell, p. 56-57.
27. Letterkenny Library; Co. Donegal, Ireland, Folklore microfilm, M.S. 1099, pp. 198-199.
28. Ibid, M.S. 1099, pp. 207-208.
29. Ó Duilearga, p. 271.
30. Uí Ógáin, pp. 197-214.
31. Wilde, Ancient Legends, pp. 29-30.

32. Devas and Men, pp. 351-358.
33. Carolan's Receipt, Manx Music For The Harp.
34. Manx Music, p. 55.
35. Bunting, pp. 105-106.
36. Mc Manus, p. 85.
37. Ó Duilearga, p. 280.
38. Hall, Paracelsus.
39. Hall, Secret Teachings.
40. Kirk, Secret Commonwealth.
41. Besant, Ancient Wisdom, p. 75.
42. Carey, p 138.
43. Latham, p. 156.
44. Evans-Wentz, The Fairy-Faith, p. 33.
45. Croker, Fairy Legends, p. viii.
46. Croker, Fairy Legends, p. 47.
47. Croker, Legends of Kerry, p. 62.
48. Folklore Department, University College Dublin, Iml. 107, p. 682.
49. Folklore Department, University College Dublin, Iml. 42, p. 190.
50. Yeats, Early Poems, pp. 80-82.
51. Yeats, Celtic Twilight, pp. 71-72.
52. Yeats, Early Poems, pp. 288-291.
53. Lenihan, p. 34.
54. Folklore Department, University College Dublin, Iml. 744, pp. 248-249.
55. Ó hEochaidh, pp. 311-313.
56. Folklore Department, University College Dublin, Iml. 485, pp. 106-107; 187-189.
57. Béaloideas, Iml. 58, 1990, p. 4.
58. Ibid, p. 23.
59. Jarrett. p. 16.
60. Hawken, p. 142.
61. Carton, pp. 49-59.
62 Crawford, pp. 133-138.
63. Mac Cana, Encyclopedia, p. 161.

FREE DETAILED CATALOGUE

A detailed illustrated catalogue is available on request, SAE or International Postal Coupon appreciated. Titles are available direct from Capall Bann, post free in the UK (cheque or PO with order) or from good bookshops and specialist outlets. Titles currently available include:

Animals, Mind Body Spirit & Folklore
Angels and Goddesses - Celtic Christianity & Paganism by Michael Howard
Arthur - The Legend Unveiled by C Johnson & E Lung
Auguries and Omens - The Magical Lore of Birds by Yvonne Aburrow
Book of the Veil The by Peter Paddon
Caer Sidhe - Celtic Astrology and Astronomy by Michael Bayley
Call of the Horned Piper by Nigel Jackson
Cats' Company by Ann Walker
Celtic Lore & Druidic Ritual by Rhiannon Ryall
Compleat Vampyre - The Vampyre Shaman: Werewolves & Witchery by Nigel Jackson
Crystal Clear - A Guide to Quartz Crystal by Jennifer Dent
Earth Dance - A Year of Pagan Rituals by Jan Brodie
Earth Harmony - Places of Power, Holiness and Healing by Nigel Pennick
Earth Magic by Margaret McArthur
Enchanted Forest - The Magical Lore of Trees by Yvonne Aburrow
Familiars - Animal Powers of Britain by Anna Franklin
Healing Homes by Jennifer Dent
Herbcraft - Shamanic & Ritual Use of Herbs by Susan Lavender & Anna Franklin
In Search of Herne the Hunter by Eric Fitch
Inner Space Workbook - Developing Counselling & Magical Skills Through the Tarot
Kecks, Keddles & Kesh by Michael Bayley
Living Tarot by Ann Walker
Magical Incenses and Perfumes by Jan Brodie
Magical Lore of Cats by Marion Davies
Magical Lore of Herbs by Marion Davies
Masks of Misrule - The Horned God & His Cult in Europe by Nigel Jackson
Mysteries of the Runes by Michael Howard
Oracle of Geomancy by Nigel Pennick
Patchwork of Magic by Julia Day
Pathworking - A Practical Book of Guided Meditations by Pete Jennings
Pickingill Papers - The Origins of Gardnerian Wicca by Michael Howard
Psychic Animals by Dennis Bardens
Psychic Self Defence - Real Solutions by Jan Brodie
Runic Astrology by Nigel Pennick
Sacred Animals by Gordon MacLellan
Sacred Grove - The Mysteries of the Forest by Yvonne Aburrow
Sacred Geometry by Nigel Pennick
Sacred Lore of Horses The by Marion Davies
Sacred Ring - Pagan Origins British Folk Festivals & Customs by Michael Howard
Seasonal Magic - Diary of a Village Witch by Paddy Slade
Secret Places of the Goddess by Philip Heselton
Talking to the Earth by Gordon Maclellan
Taming the Wolf - Full Moon Meditations by Steve Hounsome
The Goddess Year by Nigel Pennick & Helen Field
West Country Wicca by Rhiannon Ryall
Witches of Oz The by Matthew & Julia Phillips

Capall Bann is owned and run by people actively involved in many of the areas in which we publish. Our list is expanding rapidly so do contact us for details on the latest releases.

Capall Bann Publishing, Freshfields, Chieveley, Berks, RG20 8TF Tel 01635 46455